CAMP JOURNAL

NAME ....

CONTACTS: ....

CAMP: ....

DATE: ....

Week:

from: / /
to: / /

activity schedule:
MONDAY

- [ ] ------------------------------------
- [ ] ------------------------------------
- [ ] ------------------------------------

- [ ] ------------------------------------
- [ ] ------------------------------------
- [ ] ------------------------------------

- [ ] ------------------------------------
- [ ] ------------------------------------
- [ ] ------------------------------------

- [ ] ------------------------------------
- [ ] ------------------------------------
- [ ] ------------------------------------

DATE:

activity schedule:
TUESDAY

- [ ] --
- [ ] --
- [ ] --

- [ ] --
- [ ] --
- [ ] --

- [ ] --
- [ ] --
- [ ] --

- [ ] --
- [ ] --
- [ ] --

DATE:

activity schedule:
WEDNESDAY

DATE:

activity schedule:
THURSDAY

- ☐ _____
- ☐ _____
- ☐ _____

- ☐ _____
- ☐ _____
- ☐ _____

- ☐ _____
- ☐ _____
- ☐ _____

- ☐ _____
- ☐ _____
- ☐ _____

DATE:

activity schedule:
FRIDAY

- [ ] ....
- [ ] ....
- [ ] ....

- [ ] ....
- [ ] ....
- [ ] ....

- [ ] ....
- [ ] ....
- [ ] ....

- [ ] ....
- [ ] ....
- [ ] ....

DATE:

activity schedule:
SATURDAY

- [ ] --------------------------------
- [ ] --------------------------------
- [ ] --------------------------------

- [ ] --------------------------------
- [ ] --------------------------------
- [ ] --------------------------------

- [ ] --------------------------------
- [ ] --------------------------------
- [ ] --------------------------------

- [ ] --------------------------------
- [ ] --------------------------------
- [ ] --------------------------------

DATE:

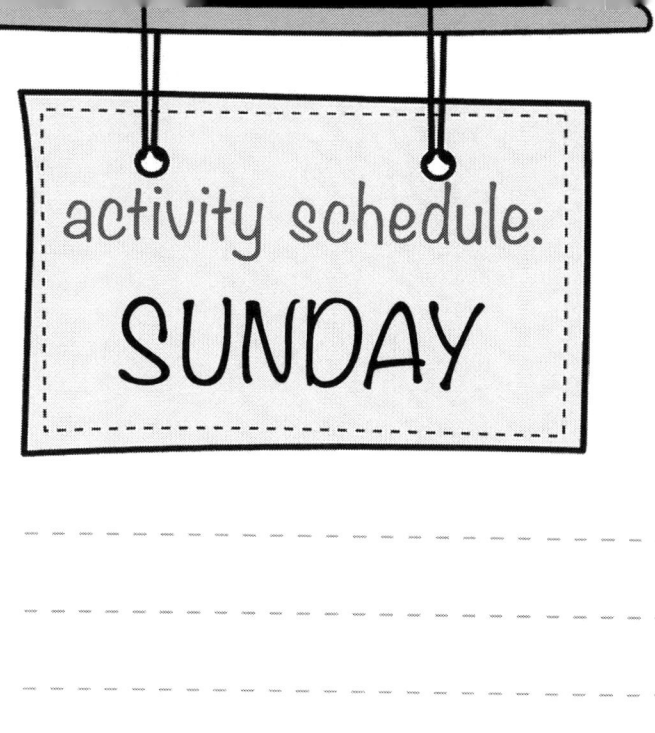

activity schedule:
SUNDAY

- [ ] ---------------------------------
- [ ] ---------------------------------
- [ ] ---------------------------------

- [ ] ---------------------------------
- [ ] ---------------------------------
- [ ] ---------------------------------

- [ ] ---------------------------------
- [ ] ---------------------------------
- [ ] ---------------------------------

- [ ] ---------------------------------
- [ ] ---------------------------------
- [ ] ---------------------------------

DATE:

MONDAY

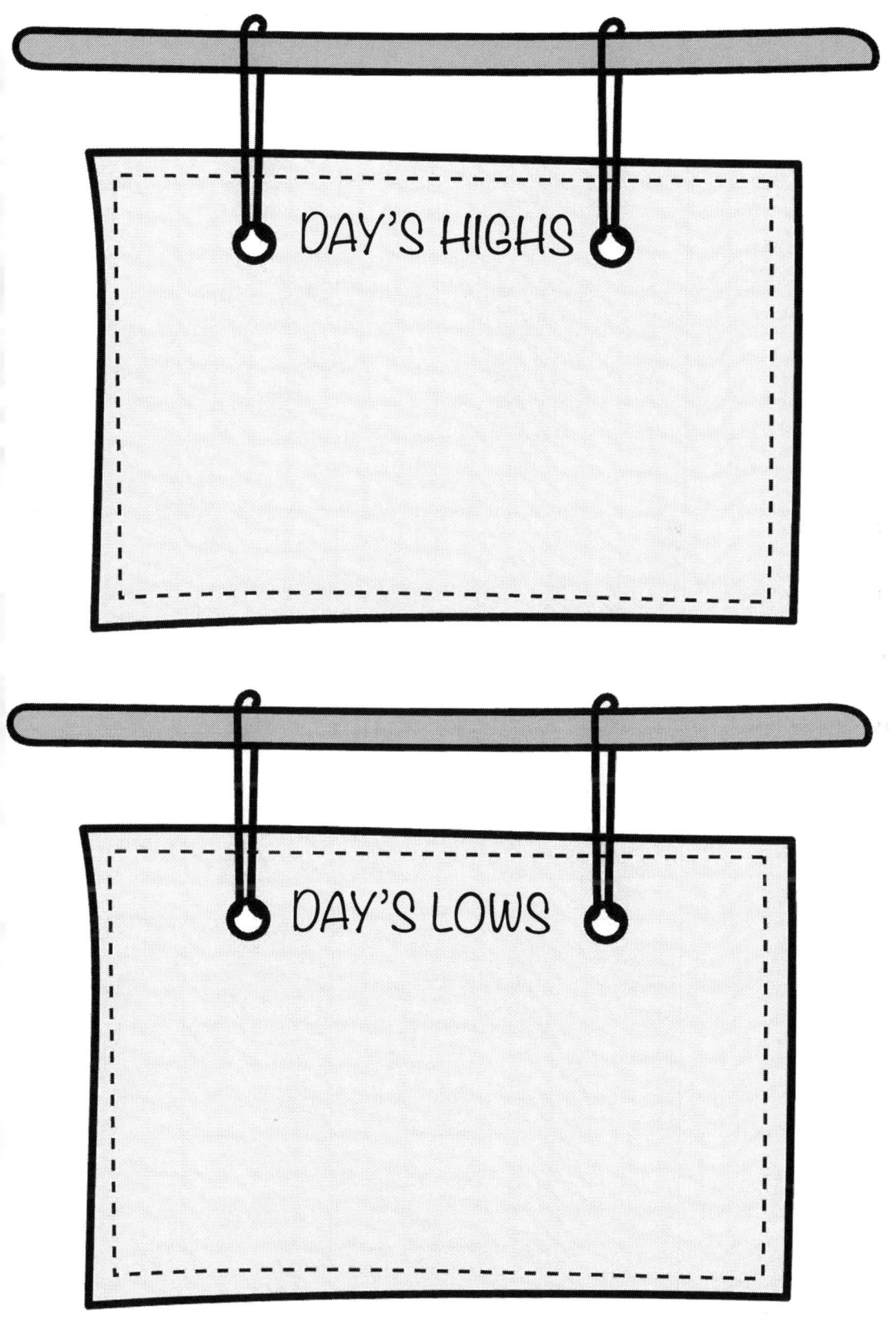

TUESDAY

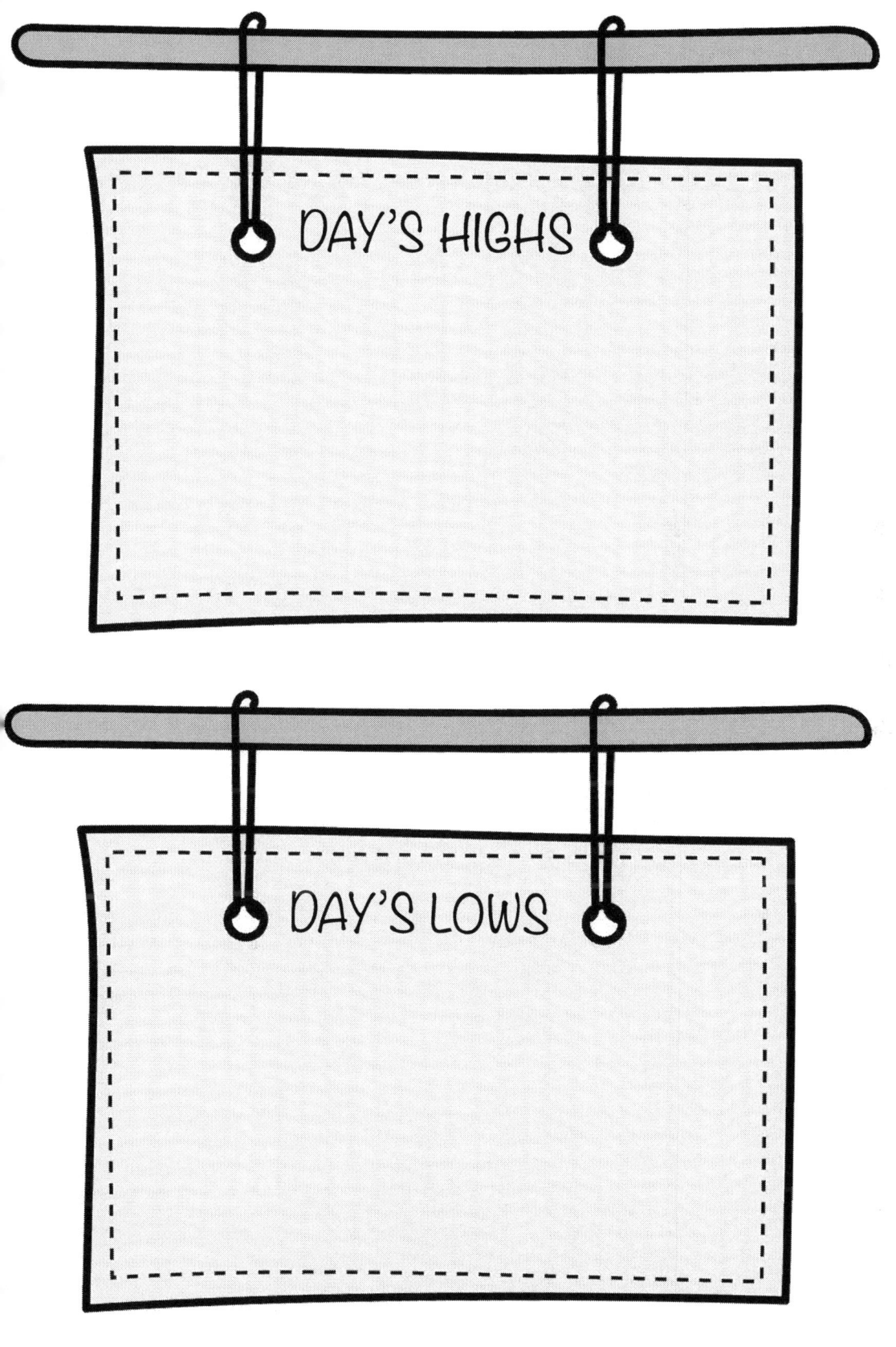

WEDNESDAY

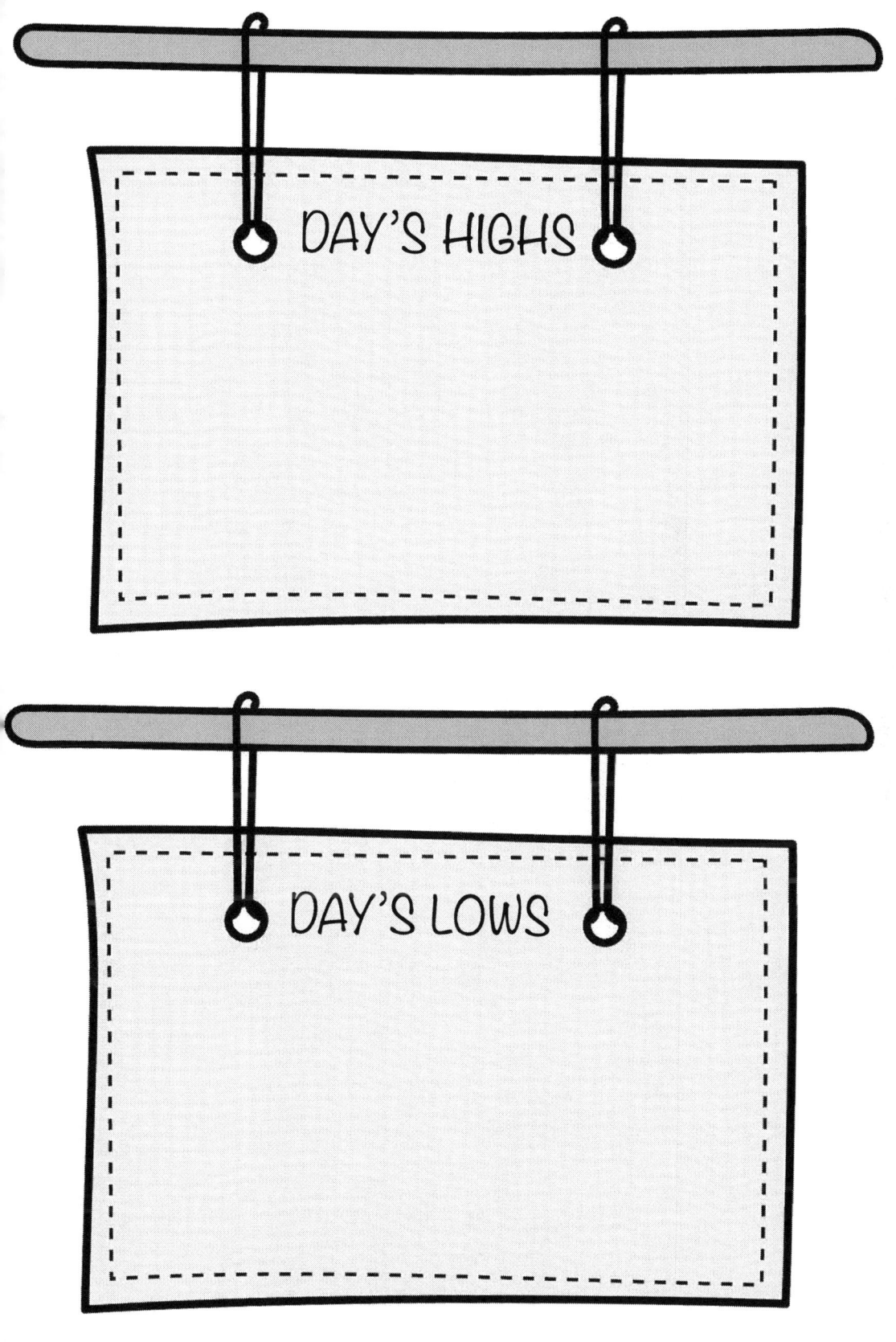

THURSDAY

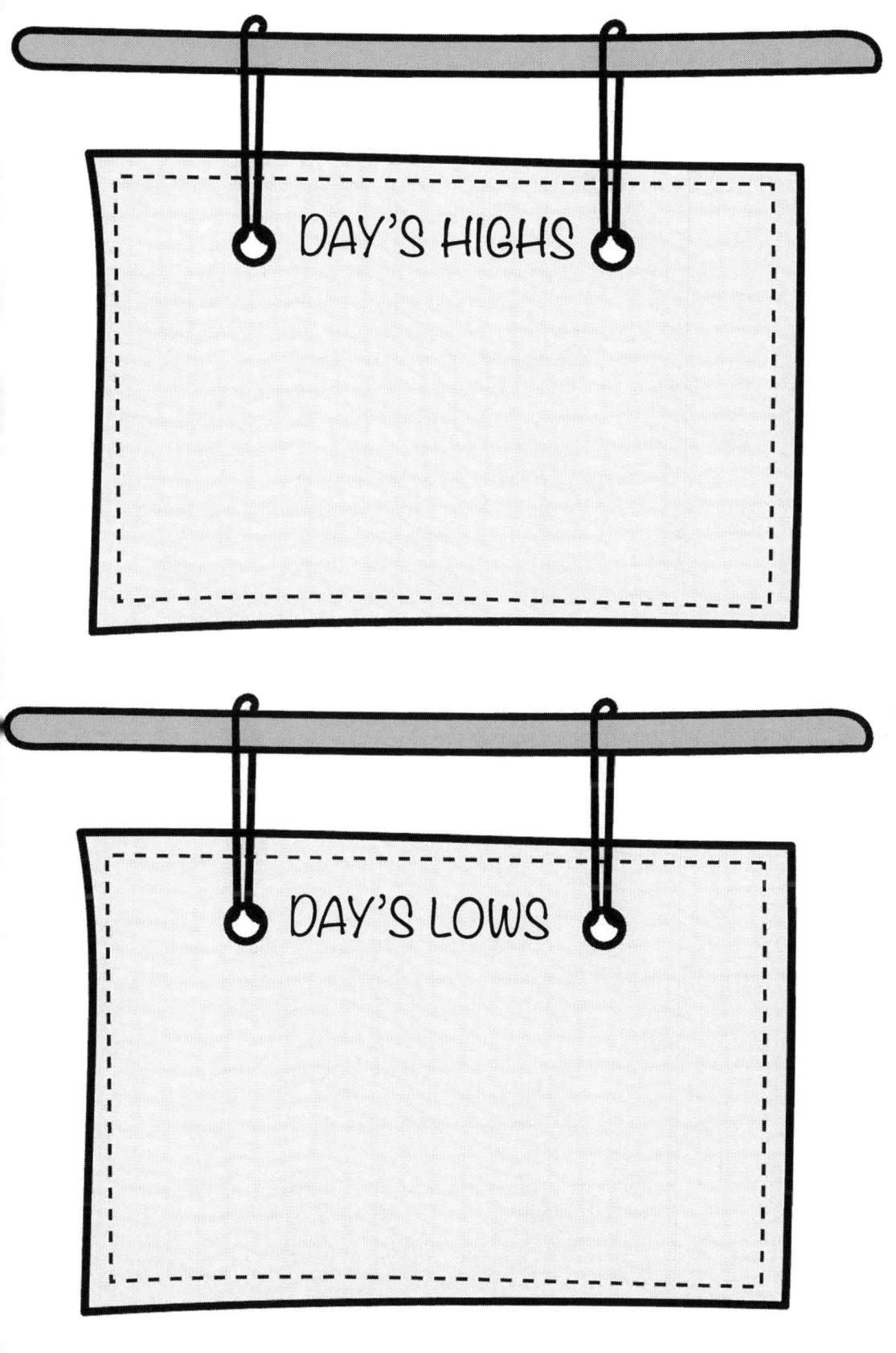

FRIDAY

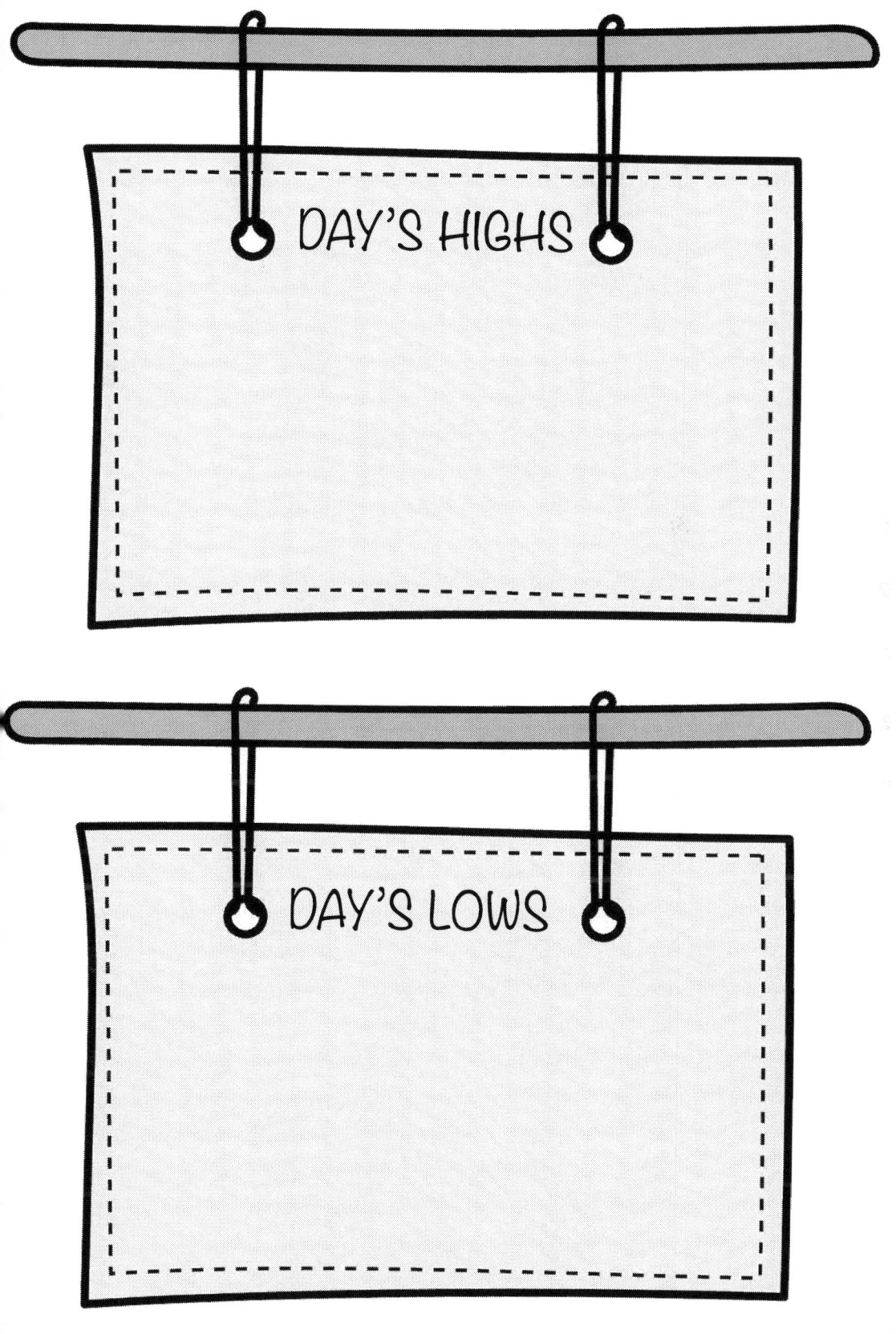

SATURDAY

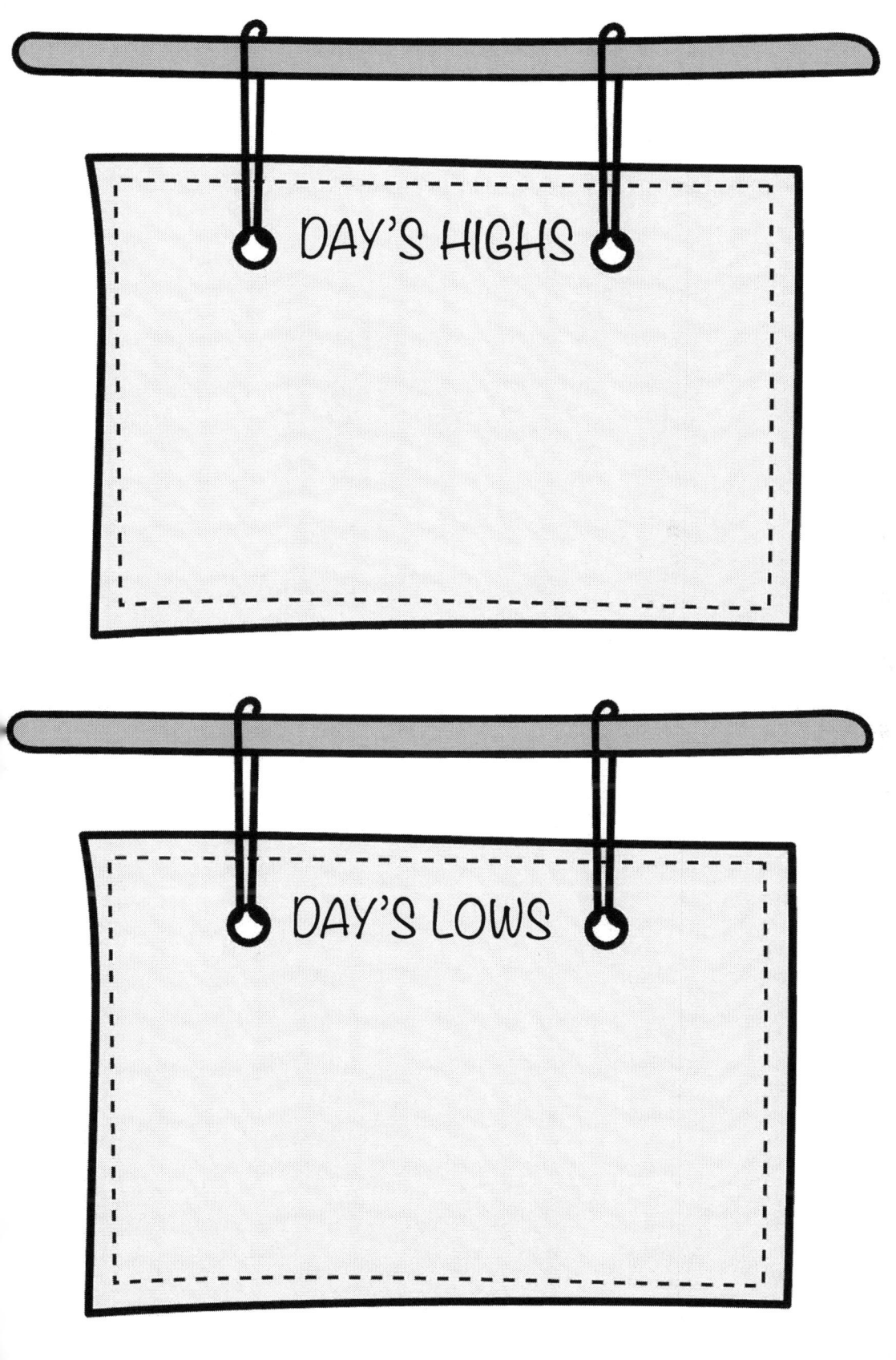

SUNDAY

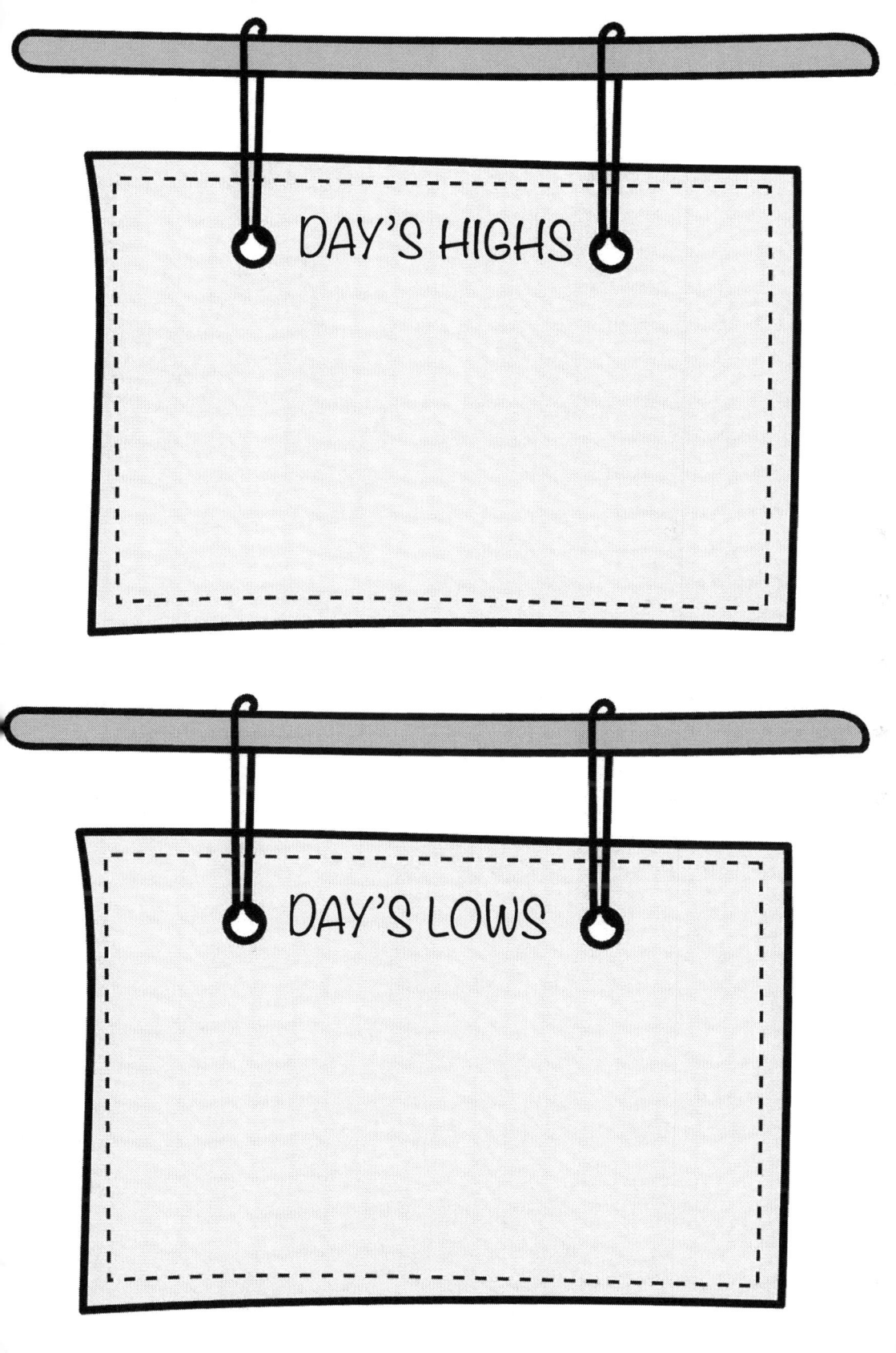

THIS WEEK

Skills learned

DRAWINGS/NOTES

AUTOGRAPHS:

AUTOGRAPHS:

DRAWINGS/NOTES

Week:

from: /   /

to: /   /

activity schedule:

MONDAY

DATE:

activity schedule:

TUESDAY

- ☐
- ☐
- ☐

- ☐
- ☐
- ☐

- ☐
- ☐
- ☐

- ☐
- ☐
- ☐

DATE:

activity schedule:
WEDNESDAY

- [ ] --
- [ ] --
- [ ] --

- [ ] --
- [ ] --
- [ ] --

- [ ] --
- [ ] --
- [ ] --

- [ ] --
- [ ] --
- [ ] --

DATE:

activity schedule:
THURSDAY

- [ ] --
- [ ] --
- [ ] --

- [ ] --
- [ ] --
- [ ] --

- [ ] --
- [ ] --
- [ ] --

- [ ] --
- [ ] --
- [ ] --

DATE:

☐ --

☐ --

☐ --

☐ --

☐ --

☐ --

☐ --

☐ --

☐ --

☐ --

☐ --

☐ --

DATE:

activity schedule:
SATURDAY

- [ ] --------------------------------
- [ ] --------------------------------
- [ ] --------------------------------

- [ ] --------------------------------
- [ ] --------------------------------
- [ ] --------------------------------

- [ ] --------------------------------
- [ ] --------------------------------
- [ ] --------------------------------

- [ ] --------------------------------
- [ ] --------------------------------
- [ ] --------------------------------

DATE:

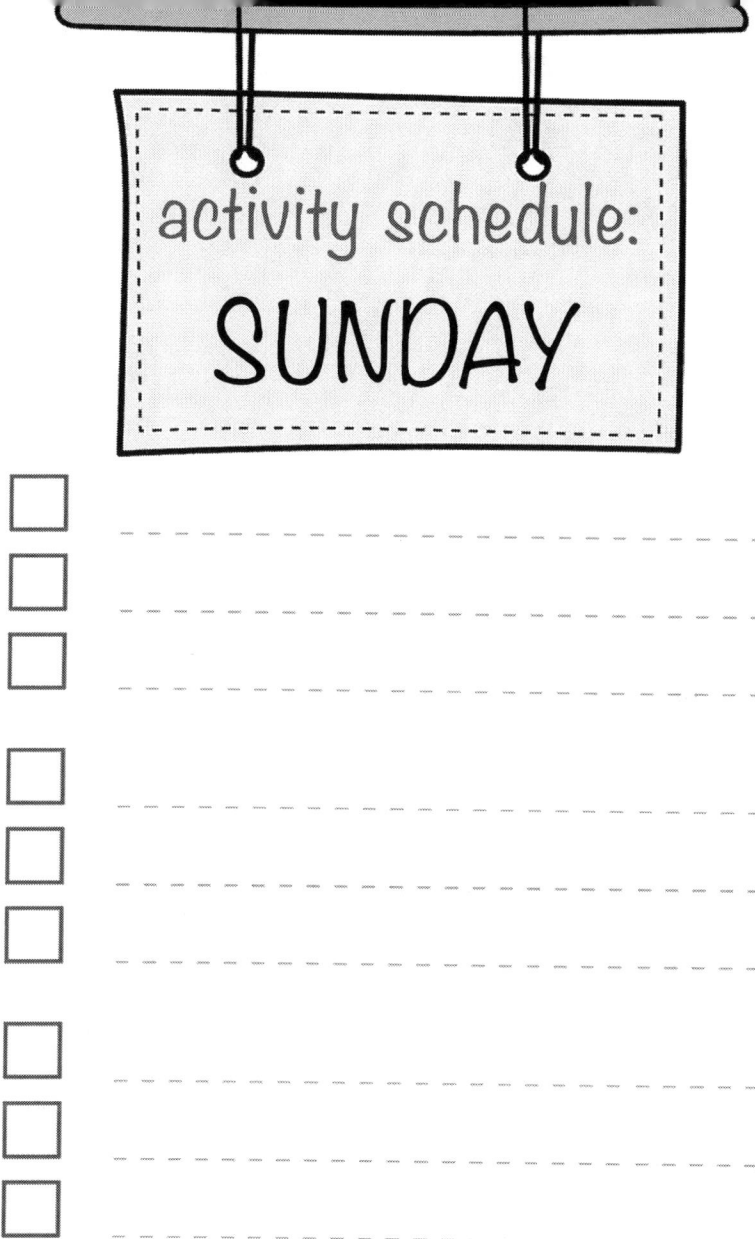

activity schedule:
SUNDAY

- ☐ --
- ☐ --
- ☐ --

- ☐ --
- ☐ --
- ☐ --

- ☐ --
- ☐ --
- ☐ --

- ☐ --
- ☐ --
- ☐ --

DATE:

MONDAY

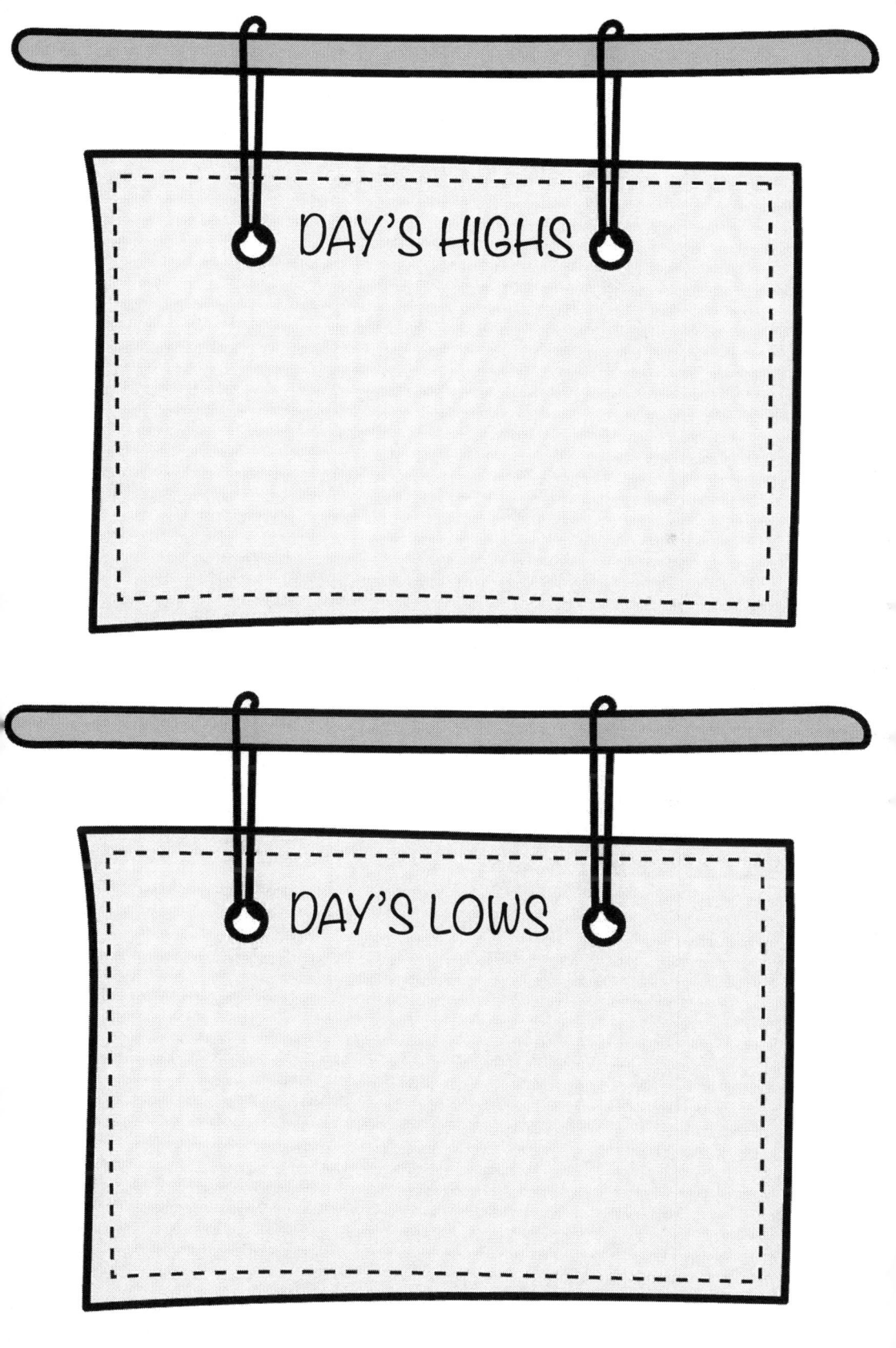

TUESDAY

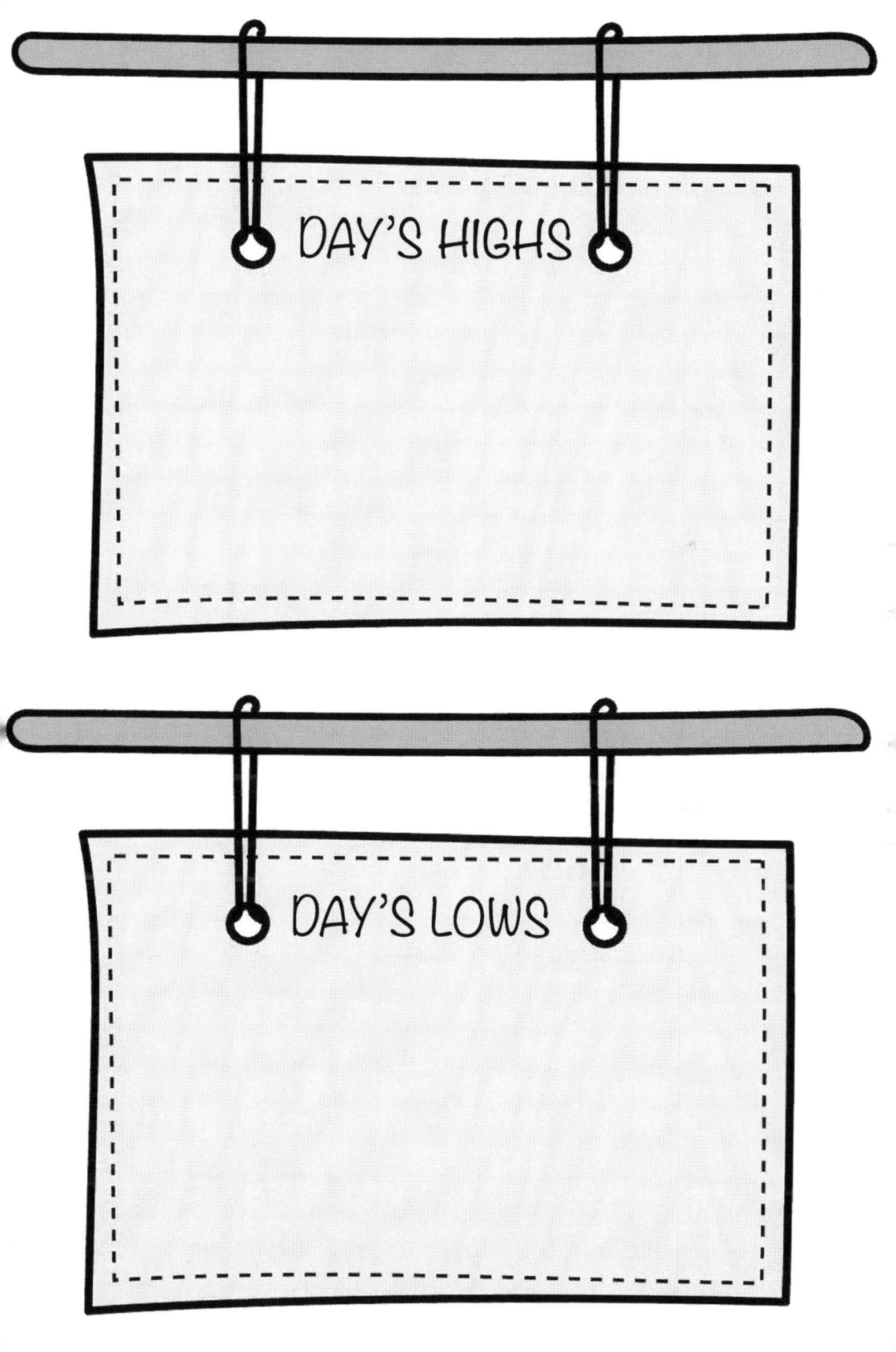

DAY'S HIGHS

DAY'S LOWS

WEDNESDAY

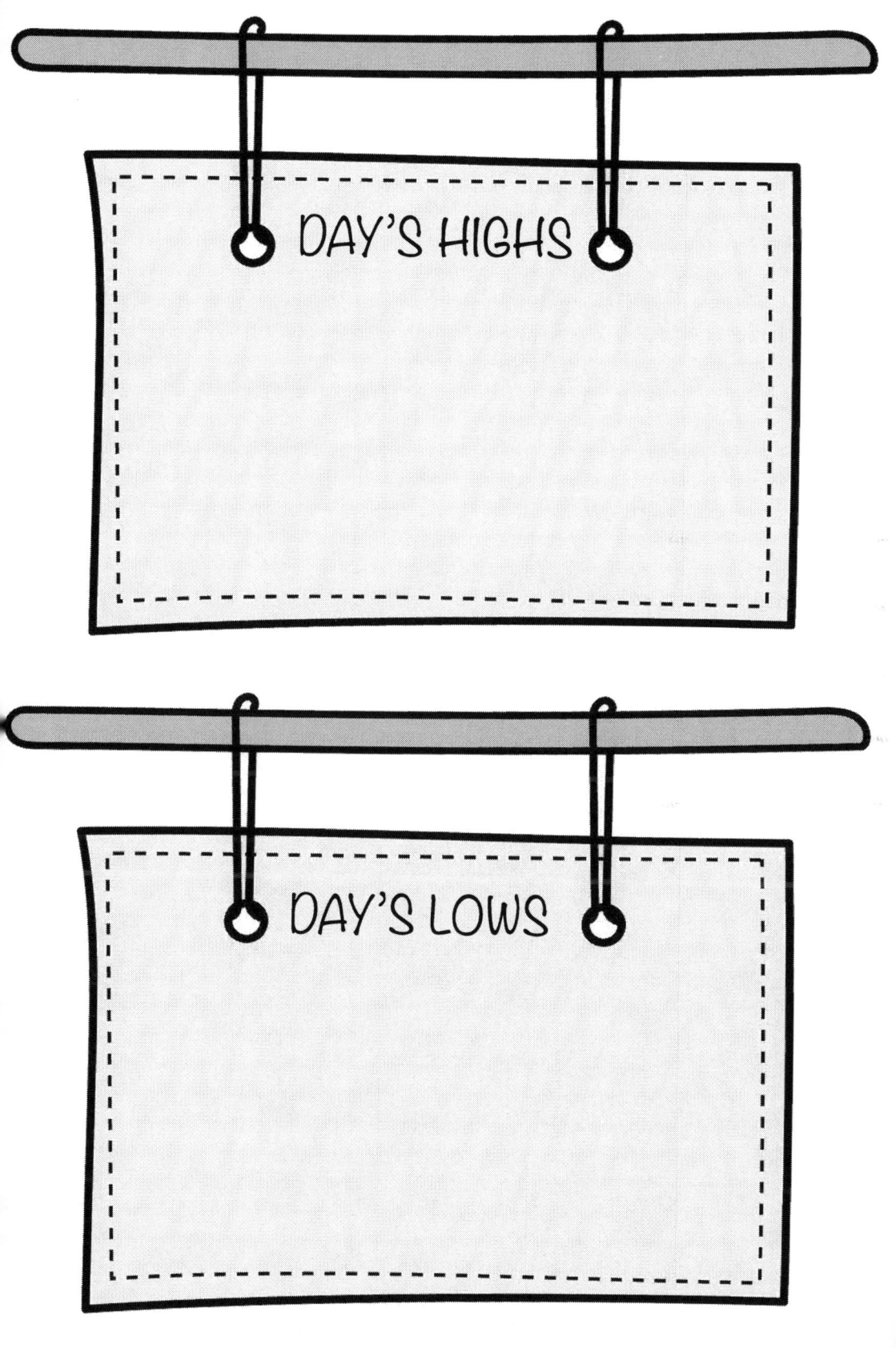

THURSDAY

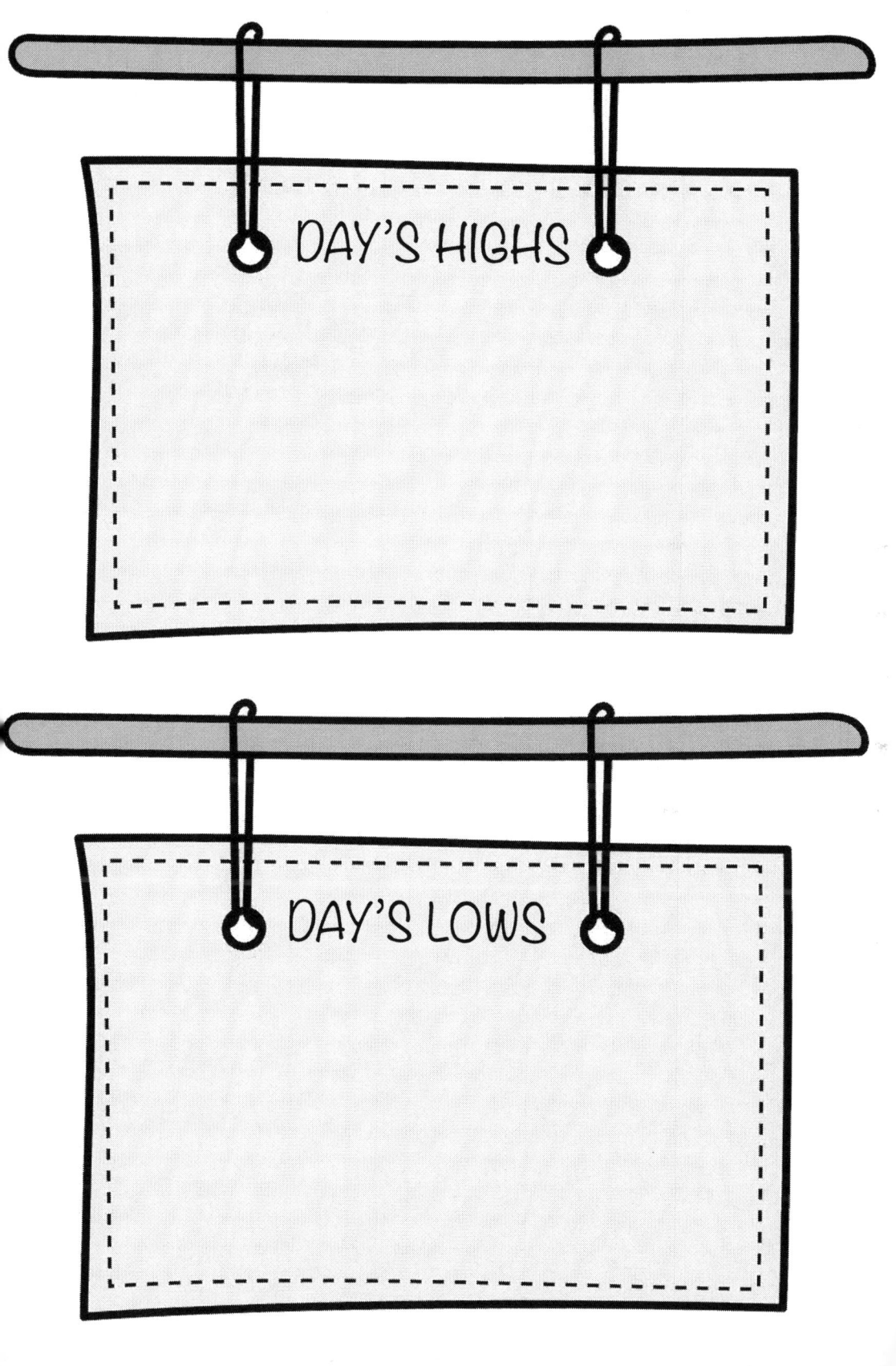

FRIDAY

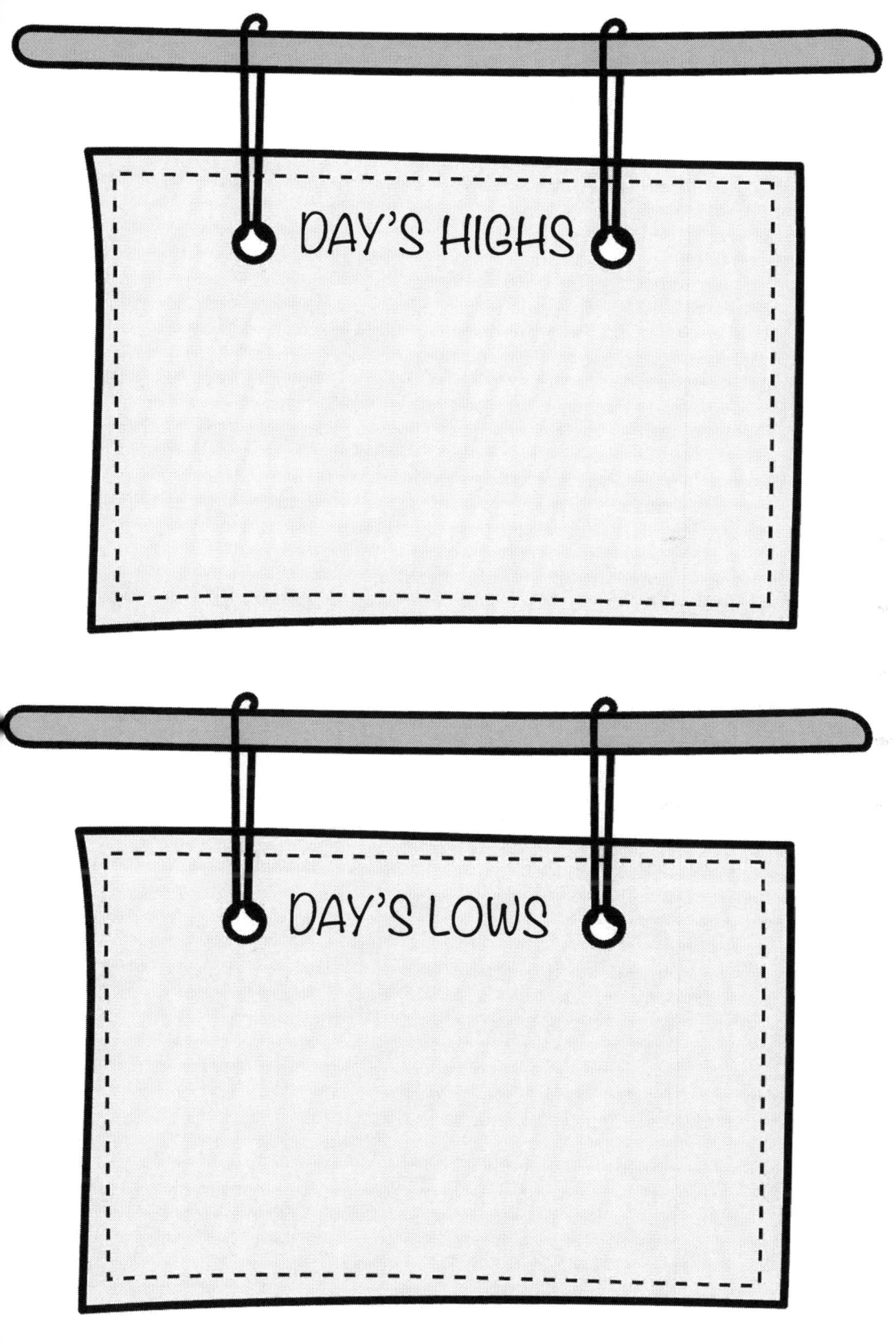

SATURDAY

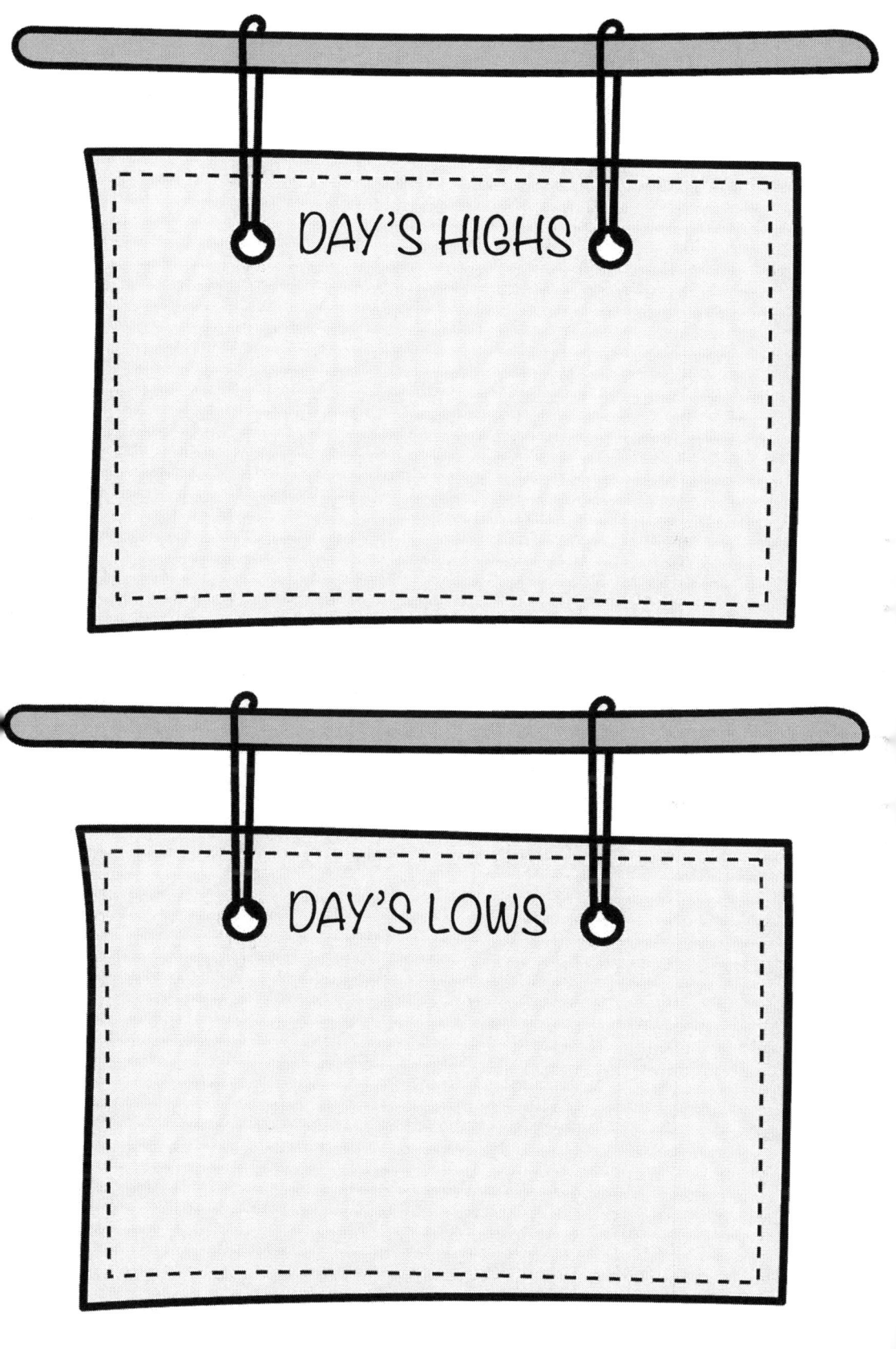

DAY'S HIGHS

DAY'S LOWS

SUNDAY

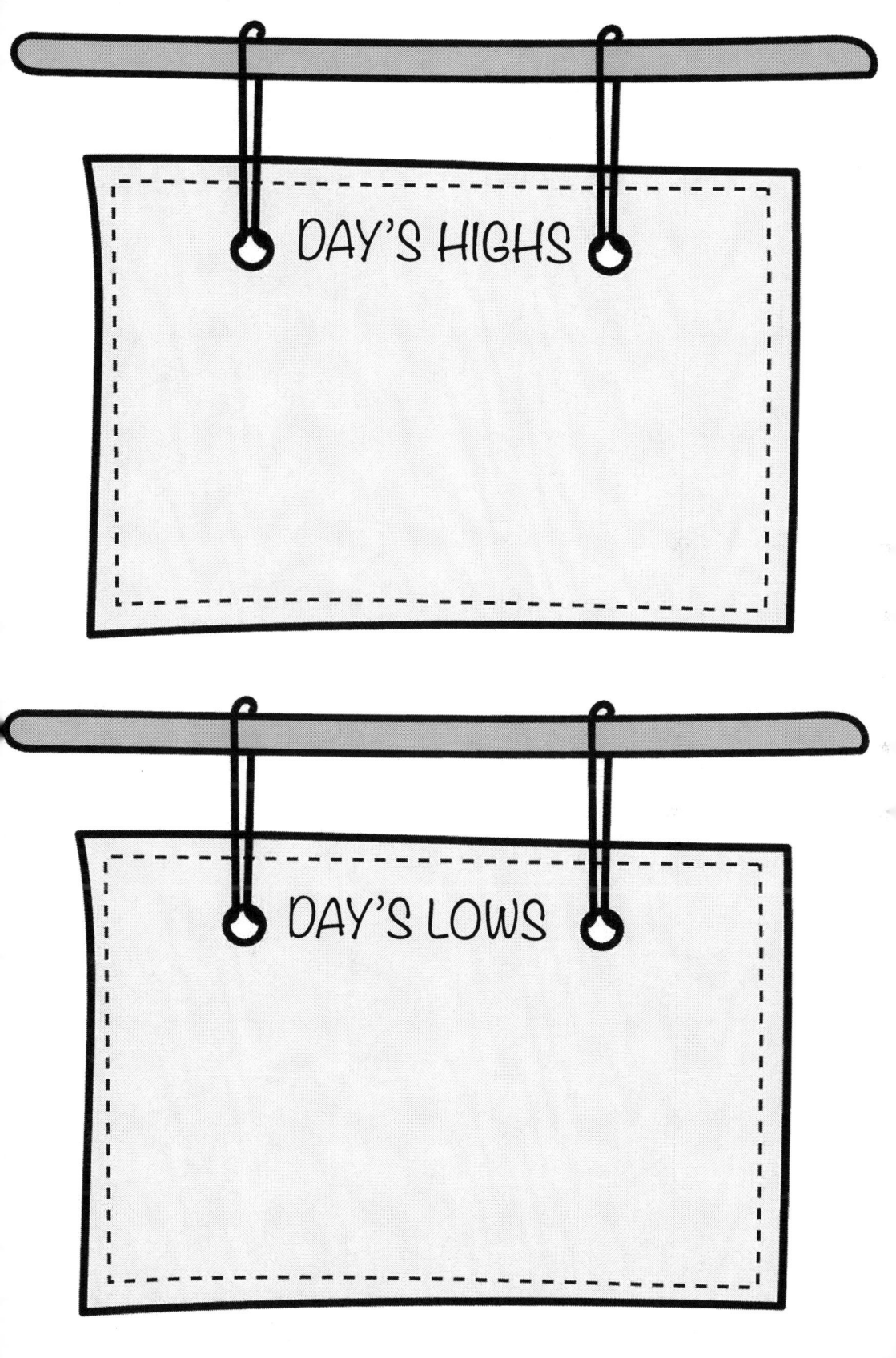

THIS WEEK

Skills learned

DRAWINGS/NOTES

AUTOGRAPHS:

AUTOGRAPHS:

DRAWINGS/NOTES

Week:

from: / /

to: / /

activity schedule:
MONODAY

DATE:

activity schedule:

TUESDAY

DATE:

activity schedule:
WEDNESDAY

☐ ---

☐ ---

☐ ---

☐ ---

☐ ---

☐ ---

☐ ---

☐ ---

☐ ---

☐ ---

☐ ---

☐ ---

DATE:

activity schedule:
THURSDAY

- [ ] --------------------------------------
- [ ] --------------------------------------
- [ ] --------------------------------------

- [ ] --------------------------------------
- [ ] --------------------------------------
- [ ] --------------------------------------

- [ ] --------------------------------------
- [ ] --------------------------------------
- [ ] --------------------------------------

- [ ] --------------------------------------
- [ ] --------------------------------------
- [ ] --------------------------------------

DATE:

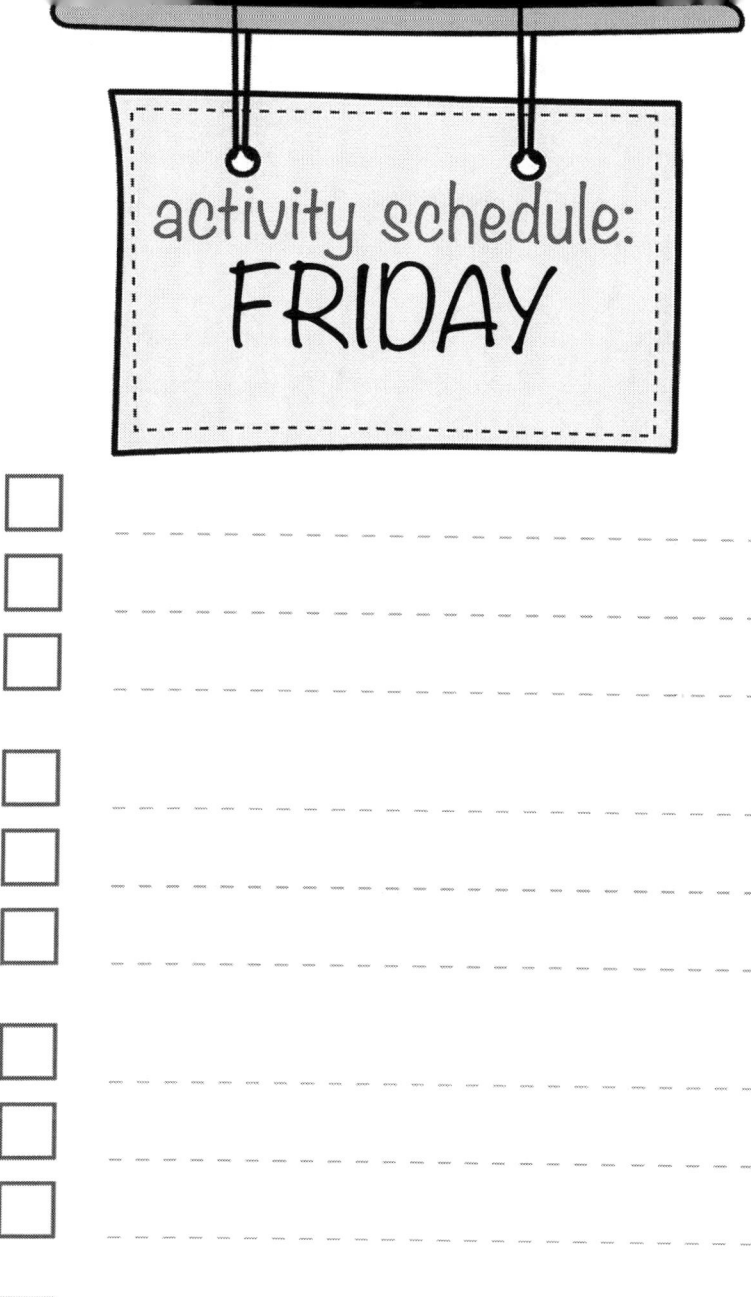

activity schedule:
FRIDAY

- [ ] ------------------------------
- [ ] ------------------------------
- [ ] ------------------------------

- [ ] ------------------------------
- [ ] ------------------------------
- [ ] ------------------------------

- [ ] ------------------------------
- [ ] ------------------------------
- [ ] ------------------------------

- [ ] ------------------------------
- [ ] ------------------------------
- [ ] ------------------------------

DATE:

activity schedule:
SATURDAY

- [ ] ----------------------------------
- [ ] ----------------------------------
- [ ] ----------------------------------

- [ ] ----------------------------------
- [ ] ----------------------------------
- [ ] ----------------------------------

- [ ] ----------------------------------
- [ ] ----------------------------------
- [ ] ----------------------------------

- [ ] ----------------------------------
- [ ] ----------------------------------
- [ ] ----------------------------------

DATE:

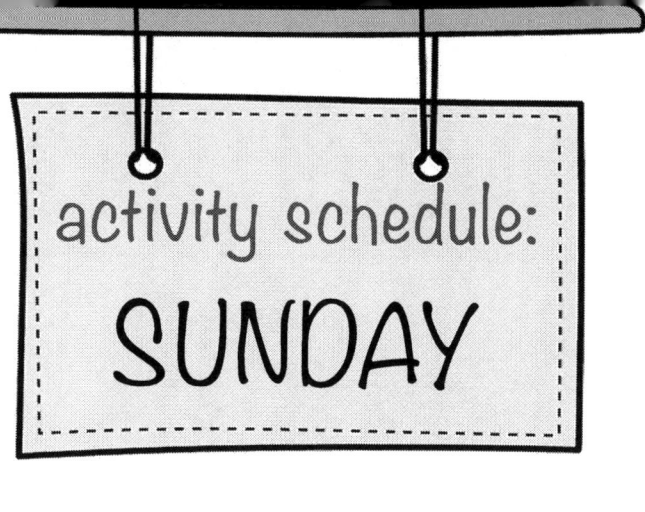

activity schedule:
SUNDAY

- ☐ ------------------------------
- ☐ ------------------------------
- ☐ ------------------------------

- ☐ ------------------------------
- ☐ ------------------------------
- ☐ ------------------------------

- ☐ ------------------------------
- ☐ ------------------------------
- ☐ ------------------------------

- ☐ ------------------------------
- ☐ ------------------------------
- ☐ ------------------------------

DATE:

MONDAY

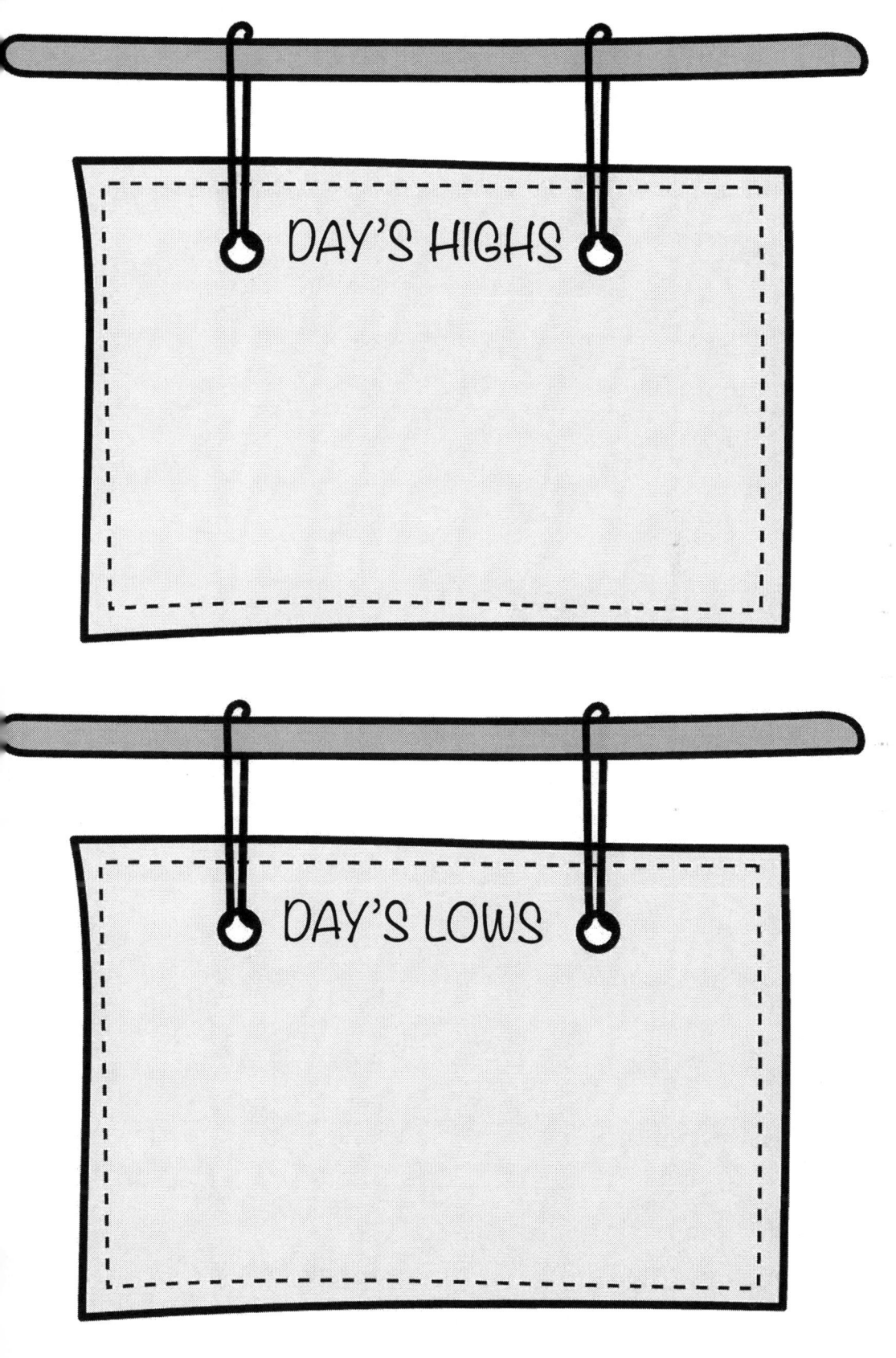

TUESDAY

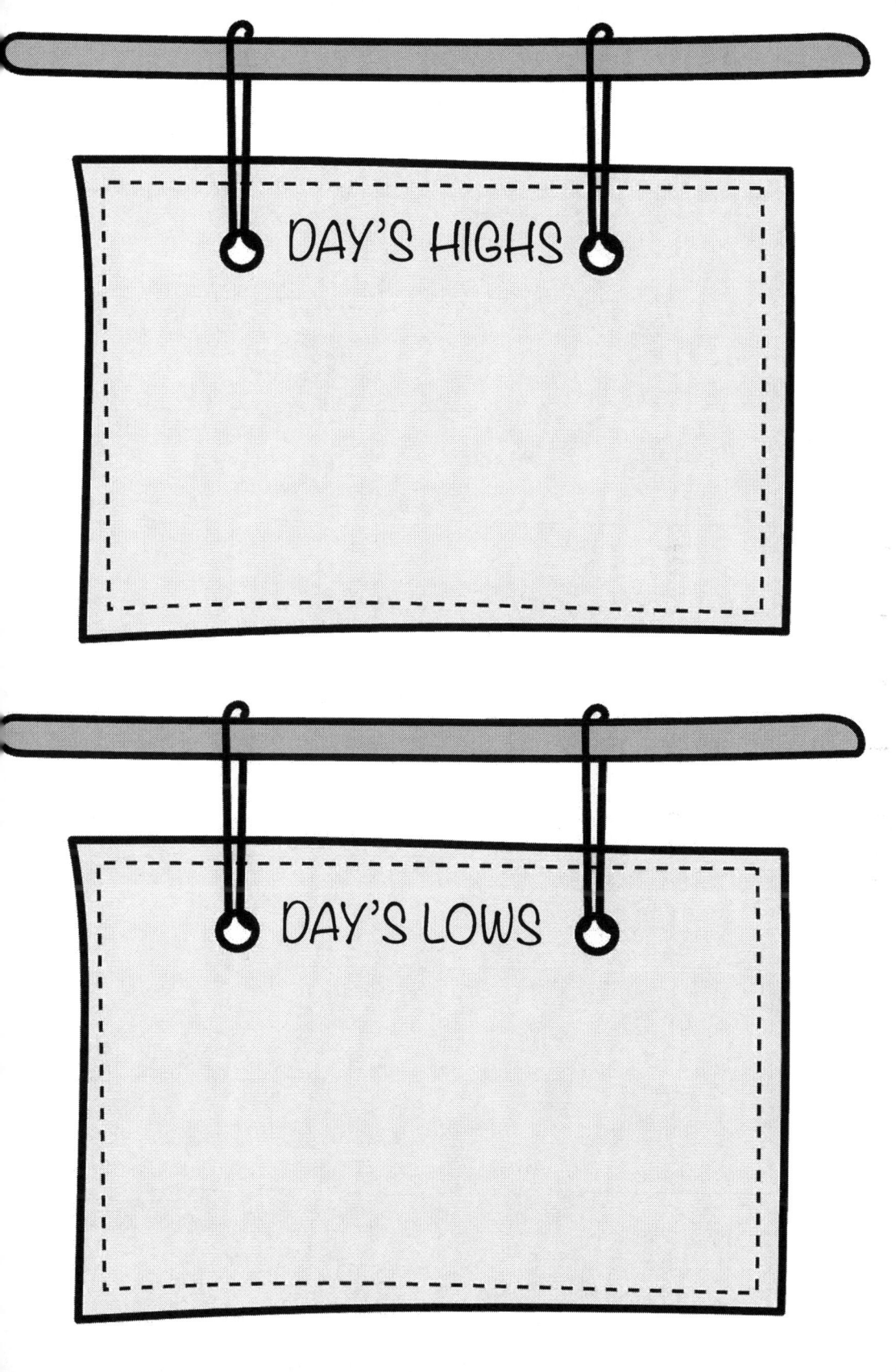

WEDNESDAY

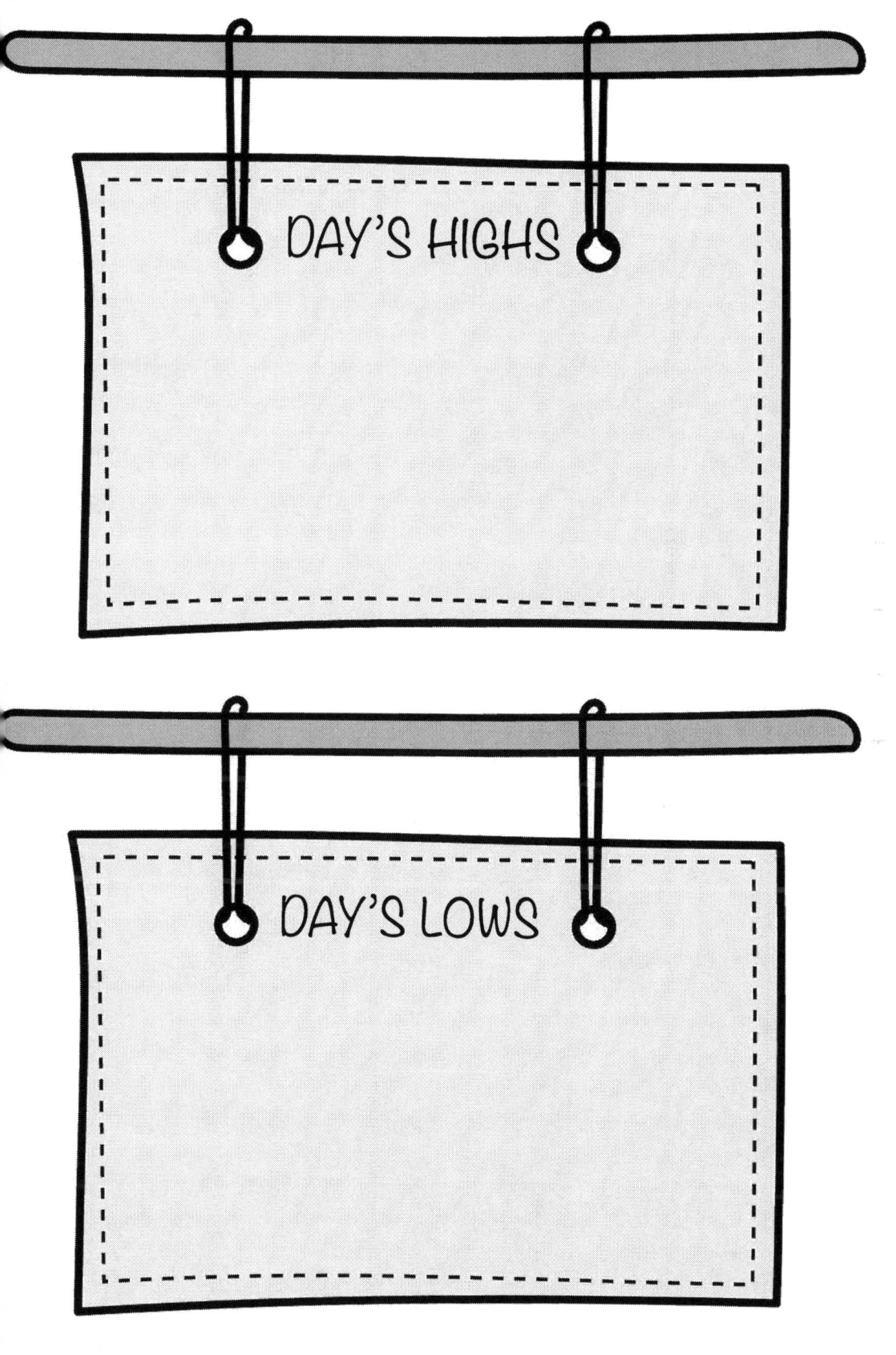

THURSDAY

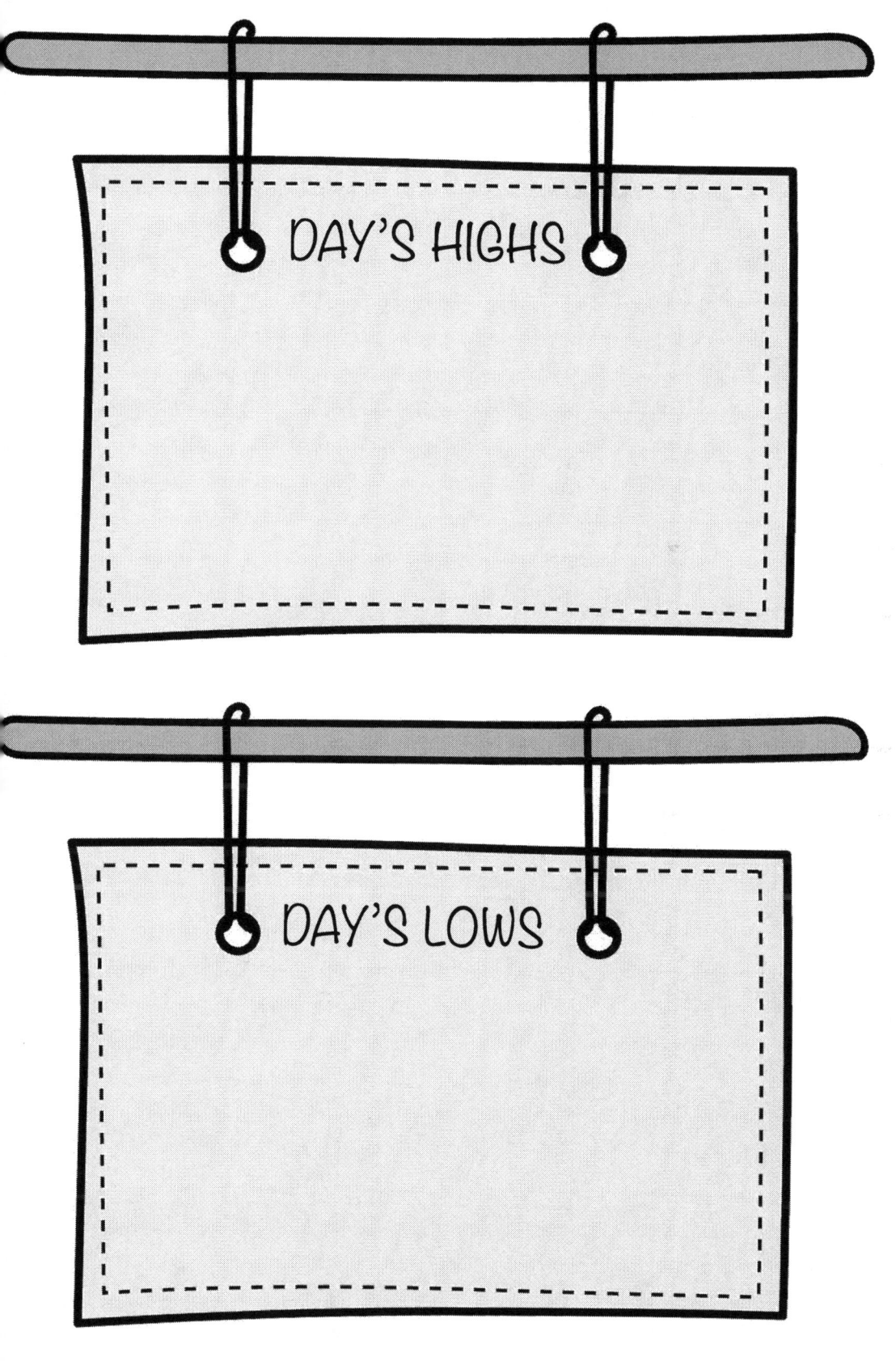

FRIDAY

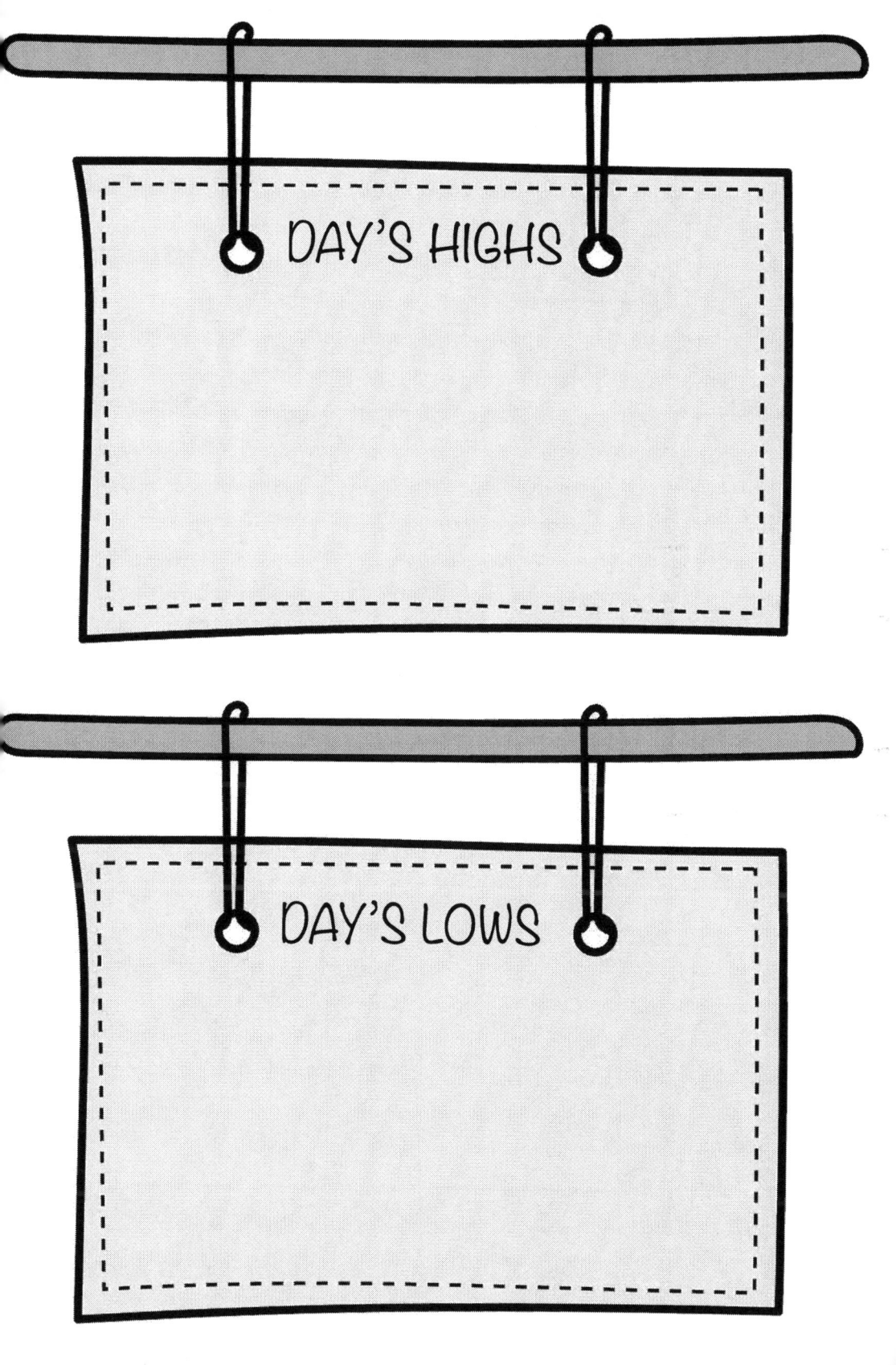

SATURDAY

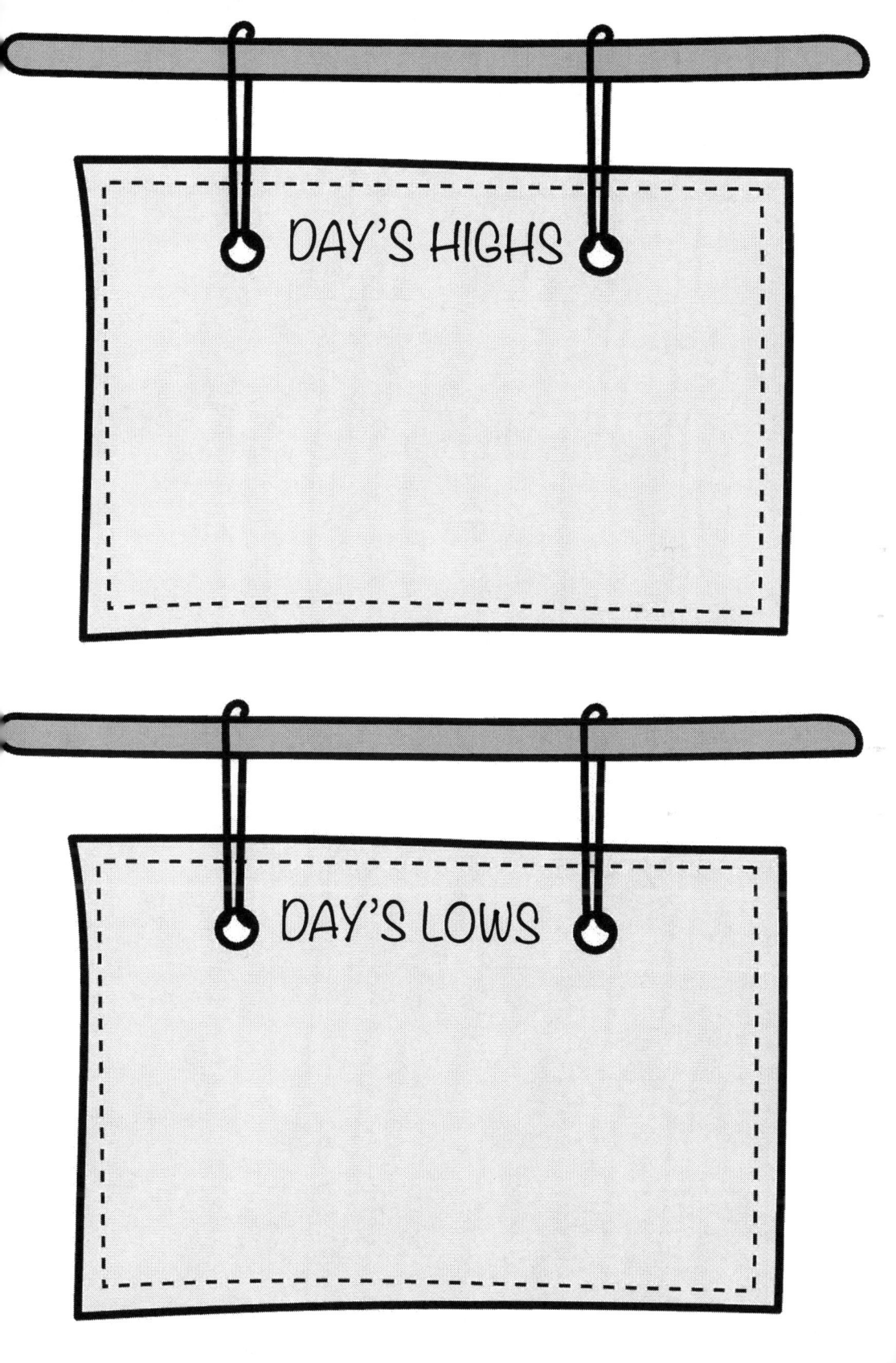

SUNDAY _____

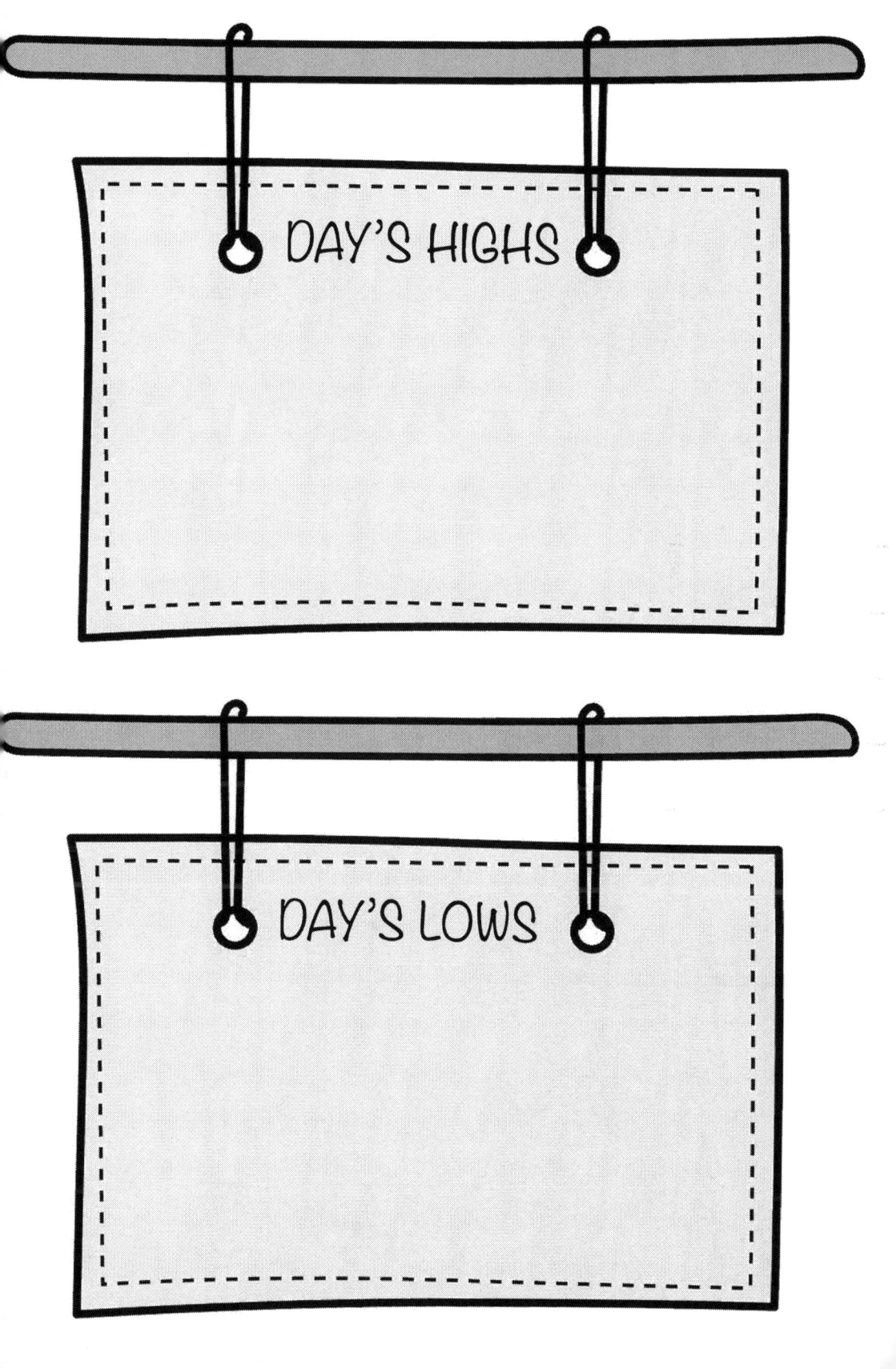

THIS WEEK

Skills learned

DRAWINGS/NOTES

AUTOGRAPHS:

AUTOGRAPHS:

DRAWINGS/NOTES

Week:

from: / /
to: / /

activity schedule:
MONDAY

- [ ] --
- [ ] --
- [ ] --

- [ ] --
- [ ] --
- [ ] --

- [ ] --
- [ ] --
- [ ] --

- [ ] --
- [ ] --
- [ ] --

DATE:

activity schedule:
TUESDAY

☐ --------------------------------
☐ --------------------------------
☐ --------------------------------

☐ --------------------------------
☐ --------------------------------
☐ --------------------------------

☐ --------------------------------
☐ --------------------------------
☐ --------------------------------

☐ --------------------------------
☐ --------------------------------
☐ --------------------------------

DATE:

activity schedule:
WEDNESDAY

- [ ]
- [ ]
- [ ]

- [ ]
- [ ]
- [ ]

- [ ]
- [ ]
- [ ]

- [ ]
- [ ]
- [ ]

DATE:

activity schedule:
THURSDAY

- [ ] _____
- [ ] _____
- [ ] _____

- [ ] _____
- [ ] _____
- [ ] _____

- [ ] _____
- [ ] _____
- [ ] _____

- [ ] _____
- [ ] _____
- [ ] _____

DATE:

activity schedule:
FRIDAY

- [ ] --------------------------------
- [ ] --------------------------------
- [ ] --------------------------------

- [ ] --------------------------------
- [ ] --------------------------------
- [ ] --------------------------------

- [ ] --------------------------------
- [ ] --------------------------------
- [ ] --------------------------------

- [ ] --------------------------------
- [ ] --------------------------------
- [ ] --------------------------------

DATE:

activity schedule:
SATURDAY

- [ ] ------------------------------
- [ ] ------------------------------
- [ ] ------------------------------

- [ ] ------------------------------
- [ ] ------------------------------
- [ ] ------------------------------

- [ ] ------------------------------
- [ ] ------------------------------
- [ ] ------------------------------

- [ ] ------------------------------
- [ ] ------------------------------
- [ ] ------------------------------

DATE:

activity schedule:
SUNDAY

- ☐ ....
- ☐ ....
- ☐ ....

- ☐ ....
- ☐ ....
- ☐ ....

- ☐ ....
- ☐ ....
- ☐ ....

- ☐ ....
- ☐ ....
- ☐ ....

DATE:

MONDAY

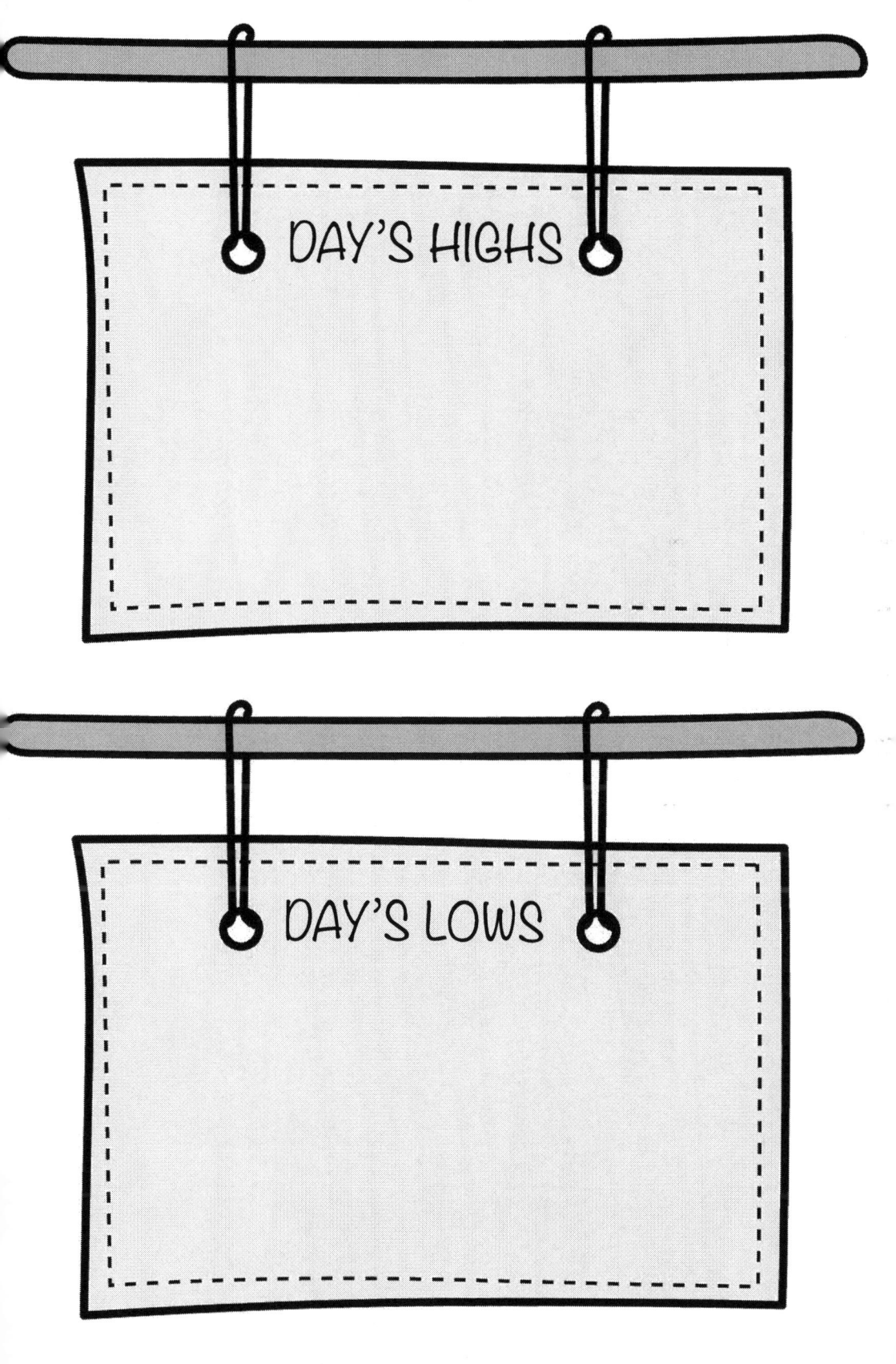

TUESDAY

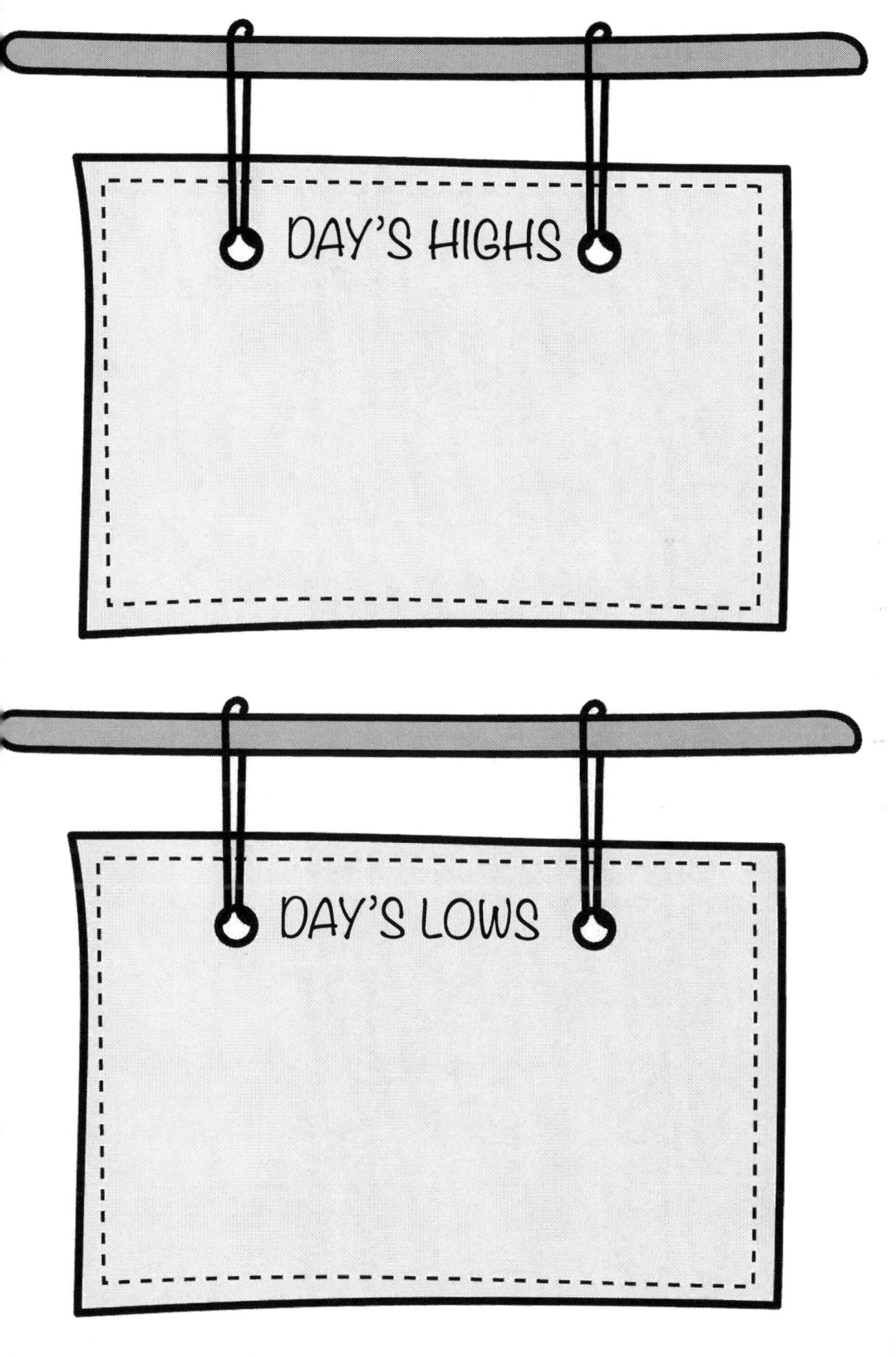

DAY'S HIGHS

DAY'S LOWS

WEDNESDAY

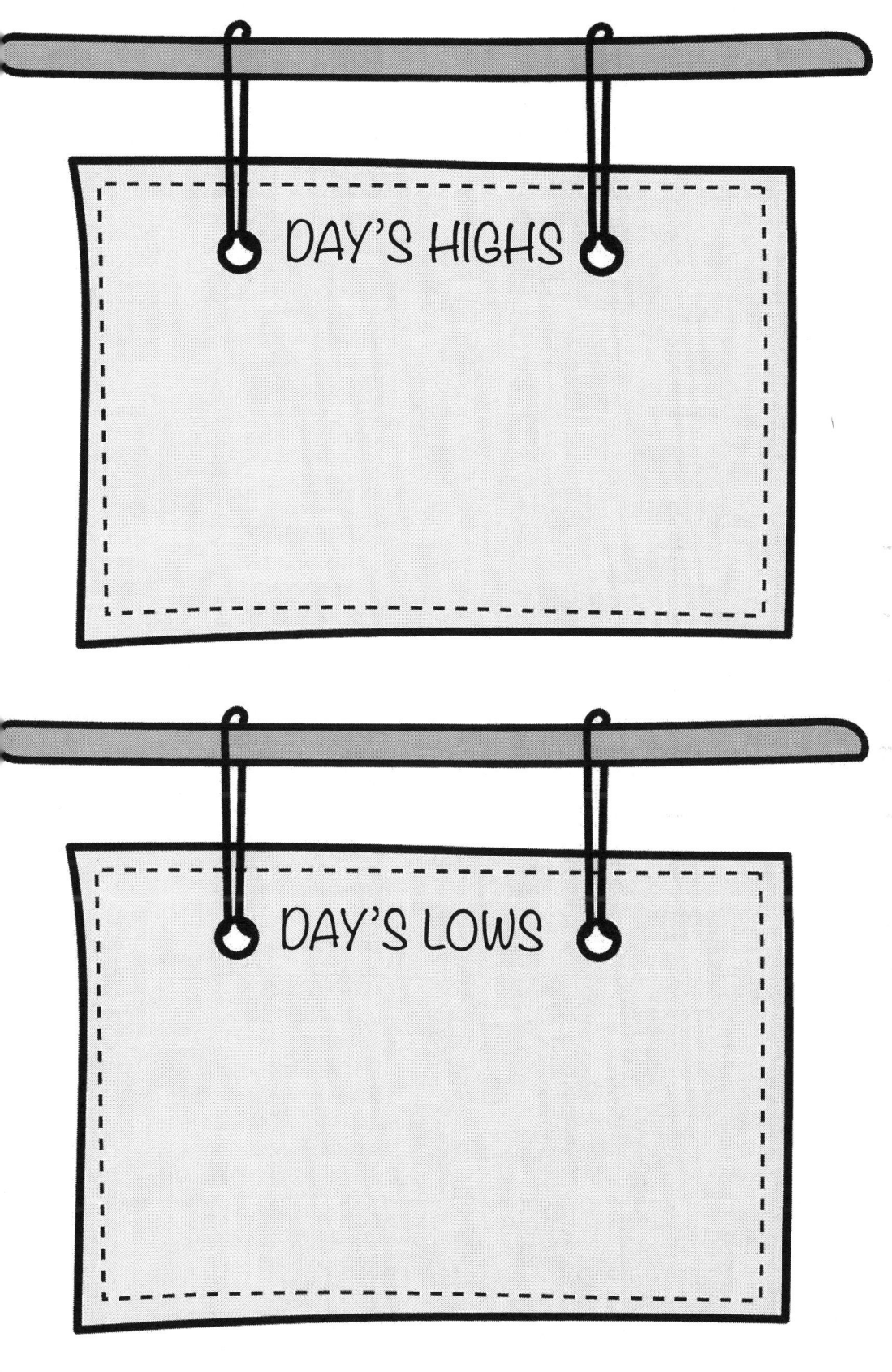

THURSDAY

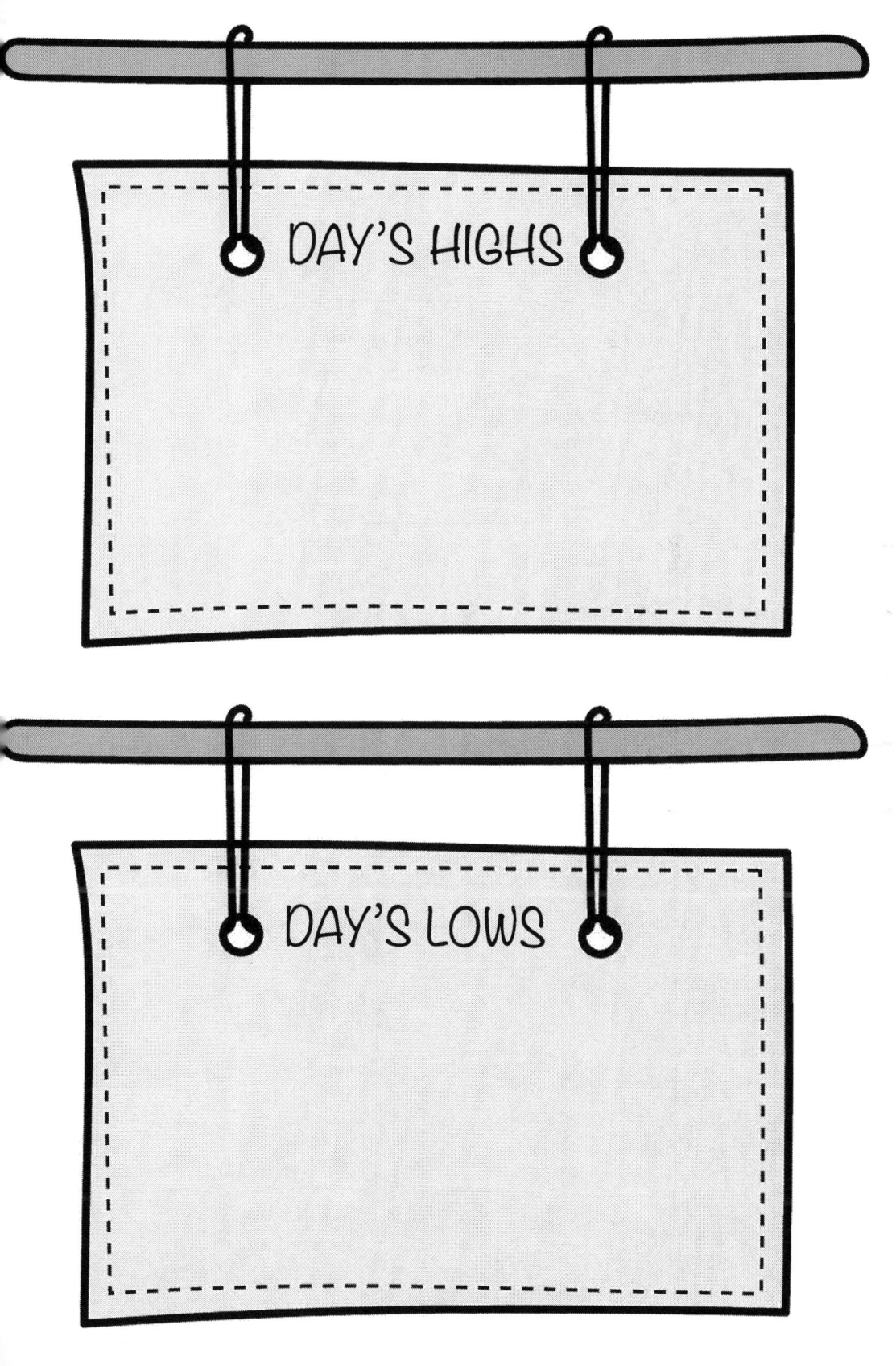

FRIDAY

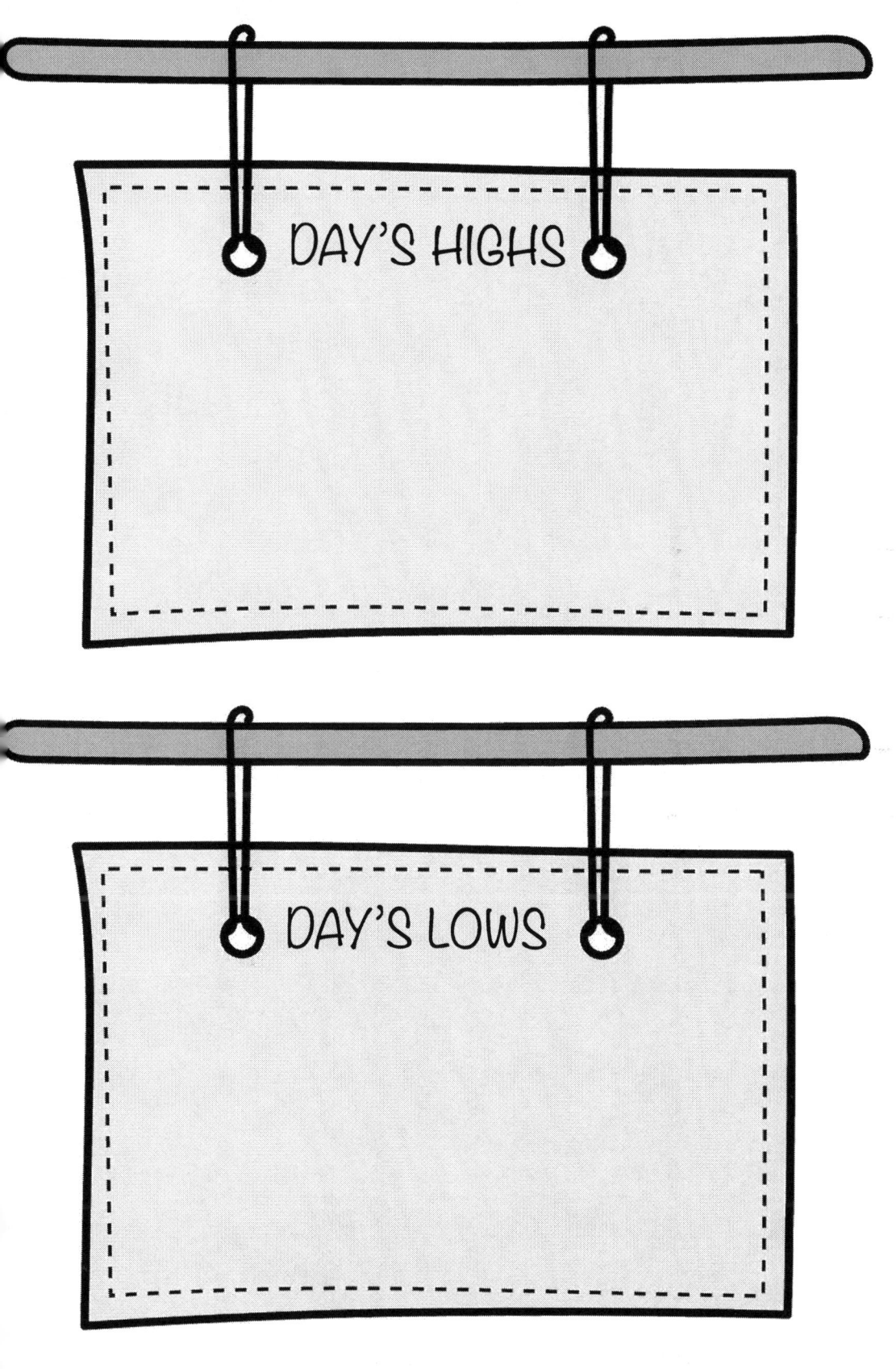

SATURDAY

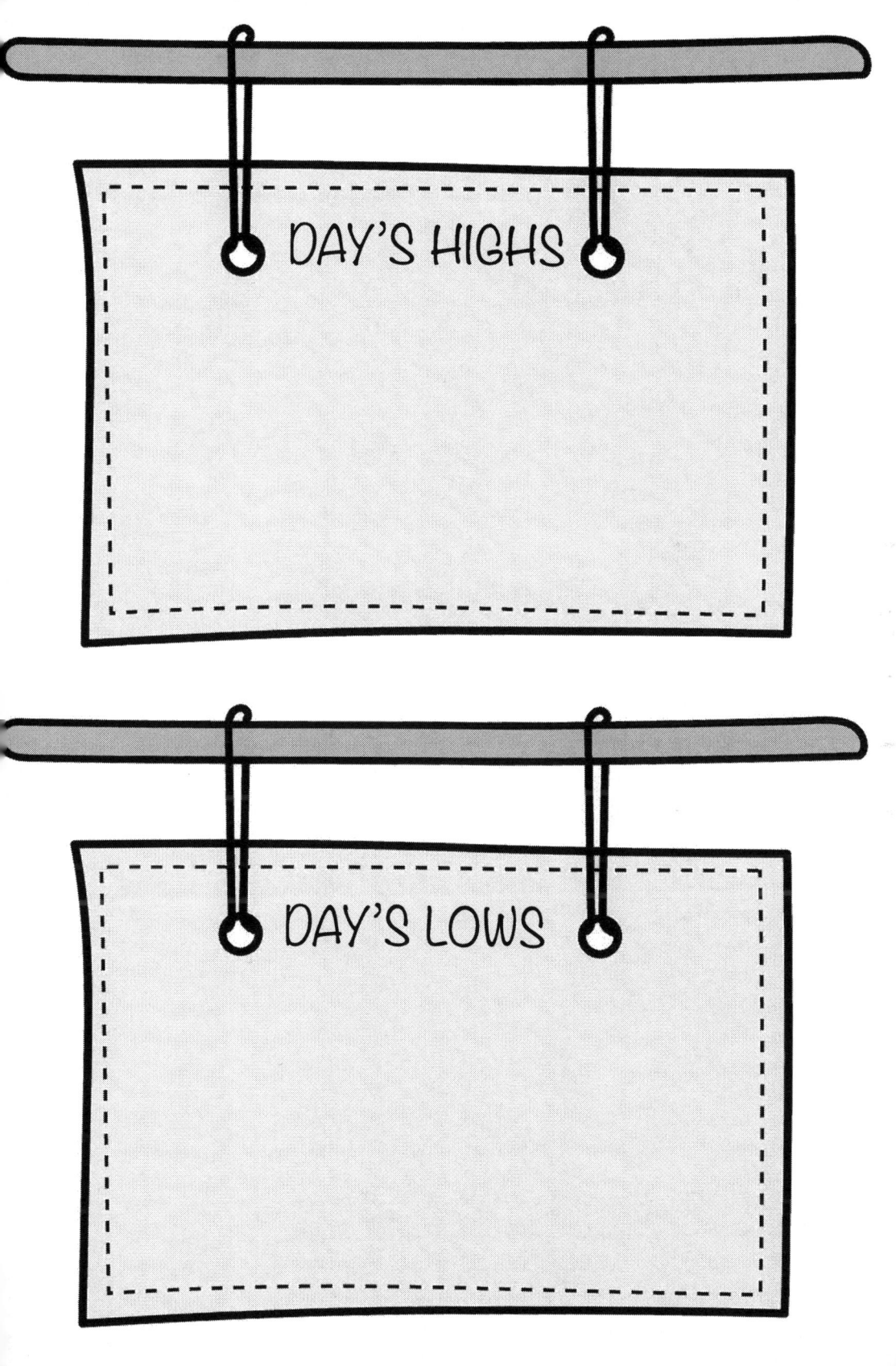

SUNDAY

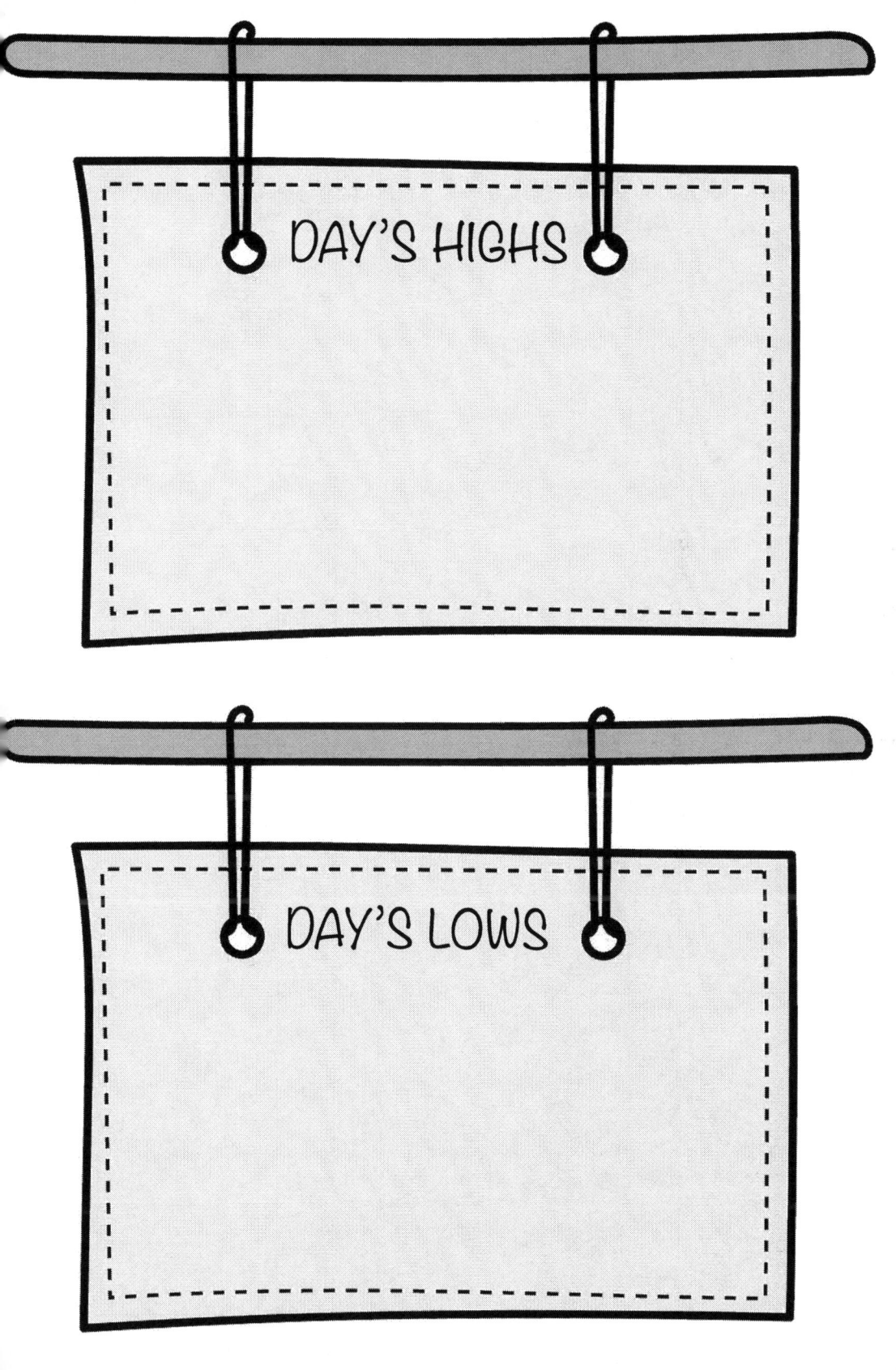

THIS WEEK

DRAWINGS/NOTES

AUTOGRAPHS:

AUTOGRAPHS:

MY BUNKMATES:

name: _____
phone: _____
address: _____
socials: _____

name: _____
phone: _____
address: _____
socials: _____

name: _____
phone: _____
address: _____
socials: _____

name: _____
phone: _____
address: _____
socials: _____

MY BUNKMATES:

name: _____
phone: _____
address: _____
socials: _____

name: _____
phone: _____
address: _____
socials: _____

name: _____
phone: _____
address: _____
socials: _____

name: _____
phone: _____
address: _____
socials: _____

MY BUNKMATES:

name: _____
phone: _____
address: _____
socials: _____

name: _____
phone: _____
address: _____
socials: _____

name: _____
phone: _____
address: _____
socials: _____

name: _____
phone: _____
address: _____
socials: _____

MY BUNKMATES:

name: _____
phone: _____
address: _____
socials: _____

name: _____
phone: _____
address: _____
socials: _____

name: _____
phone: _____
address: _____
socials: _____

name: _____
phone: _____
address: _____
socials: _____

MY BUNKMATES:

name: _____

phone: _____

address: _____

socials: _____

name: _____

phone: _____

address: _____

socials: _____

name: _____

phone: _____

address: _____

socials: _____

name: _____

phone: _____

address: _____

socials: _____

MY BUNKMATES:

name: _____

phone: _____

address: _____

socials: _____

name: _____

phone: _____

address: _____

socials: _____

name: _____

phone: _____

address: _____

socials: _____

name: _____

phone: _____

address: _____

socials: _____

MY BUNKMATES:

name: _____

phone: _____

address: _____

socials: _____

name: _____

phone: _____

address: _____

socials: _____

name: _____

phone: _____

address: _____

socials: _____

name: _____

phone: _____

address: _____

socials: _____

MY BUNKMATES:

name: _____
phone: _____
address: _____
socials: _____

name: _____
phone: _____
address: _____
socials: _____

name: _____
phone: _____
address: _____
socials: _____

name: _____
phone: _____
address: _____
socials: _____

AUTOGRAPHS:

AUTOGRAPHS:

AUTOGRAPHS:

AUTOGRAPHS:

DRAWINGS/NOTES

DRAWINGS/NOTES

DRAWINGS/NOTES

DRAWINGS/NOTES

DRAWINGS/NOTES

46130517R00072

Made in the USA
Lexington, KY
23 July 2019